ARTHURIAN STUDIES LXXVIII

CHRÉTIEN DE TROYES IN PROSE
THE BURGUNDIAN *EREC* AND *CLIGÉS*

ARTHURIAN STUDIES

ISSN 0261–9814

General Editor: Norris J. Lacy

Previously published volumes in the series
are listed at the back of this book

CHRÉTIEN DE TROYES IN PROSE
THE BURGUNDIAN
EREC AND *CLIGÉS*

Translated by
Joan Tasker Grimbert and Carol J. Chase

D. S. BREWER

First published 2011
D. S. Brewer, Cambridge

ISBN 978 1 84384 269 9

D. S. Brewer is an imprint of Boydell & Brewer Ltd
PO Box 9, Woodbridge, Suffolk, IP12 3DF, UK
and of Boydell & Brewer Inc.
668 Mount Hope Ave, Rochester, NY 14620, USA
website: www.boydellandbrewer.com

The publisher has no responsibility for the continued existence or
accuracy of URLs for external or third-party internet websites referred to
in this book, and does not guarantee that any content on such websites is,
or will remain, accurate or appropriate.

A CIP catalogue record for this book is available
from the British Library

Papers used by Boydell & Brewer Ltd are natural, recyclable products
made from wood grown in sustainable forests

Printed and bound in Great Britain by
The MPG Books Group, Bodmin and King's Lynn

Contents

For RJS and JMC

Acknowledgements

We have received a great deal of help and encouragement in the course of producing this book. Norris J. Lacy, General Editor of the Arthurian Studies series, was the first to suggest to us that an English translation of the prose *Erec* and *Cligés* would appeal to all those drawn to fifteenth-century romance and the reception of Chrétien's works. We have been most fortunate to have at our disposal the excellent critical editions of Maria Colombo Timelli, who has taken a lively interest in our project since its inception. The entire Boydell & Brewer team, starting with Caroline Palmer, has been extremely supportive throughout; we also appreciate the assistance and advice of Rohais Haughton and Vanda Andrews and the skills of Matthew Seal, Humphrey Barber, and especially Glenda Pattenden, who designed the beautiful jacket. It is a great pleasure to acknowledge the material support of both of our home institutions, The Catholic University of America and Knox College. The library directors and staff of both universities merit special thanks for facilitating our work; Sharon Clayton deserves particular mention. Finally, we are grateful for the boundless patience and loving encouragement of our respective husbands, Robert J. Smarz and Jean-Michel Comte, to whom this book is dedicated.

JTG & CJC

Introduction

From Chrétien de Troyes to the court of Philip the Good: from verse to prose

In the late twelfth century, Chrétien de Troyes composed several Arthurian romances of such quality and influence that he is considered the creator of that genre: *Erec et Enide*, *Cligés*, *Le Chevalier de la charrrette (Lancelot)*, *Le Chevalier au lion (Yvain)*, and *Le Conte du Graal (Le Roman de Perceval)*.[1] Like most writers of this period, Chrétien composed his romances in verse; his last work, *Le Conte du Graal*, which breaks off in the middle of an episode, was provided with four verse continuations, all of which date to the thirteenth century and were designed to bring closure to the tale. While authors continued to write in verse from the thirteenth century on, prose became more and more the medium of choice for narrative works, owing in part to the influence of the numerous chronicles and to the feeling that prose conveyed a greater sense of veracity than verse.

Chrétien's romances survive in manuscripts prepared mostly in the thirteenth and fourteenth centuries; his *Chevalier de la charrette*, rendered into prose, was adapted to fit into the enormously popular *Lancelot*, part of the *Lancelot-Grail Cycle*. This five-part Cycle, written in the first part of the thirteenth century, also develops material about the Grail that Chrétien had included in his *Conte du Graal*. Part of Chrétien's legacy was thus transformed early on in order to respond to the needs of a new public. His verse works coexisted with the increasingly popular prose romances. But by the fifteenth century, Chrétien's Old French verse was no longer being copied, and because the language had evolved to the stage that linguists call Middle French,[2] scholars have assumed that readers who were still interested in his romances must have found them difficult to decipher. Indeed, the evolution of the language is one of the reasons cited for the appearance in this late medieval period of prose transcriptions of some of Chrétien's works. Recently, however, Maria Colombo Timelli has nuanced this judgment. Her research suggests that the authors of mid-fifteenth-century prose renditions

---

[1] Chrétien was also one of the first *trouvères*, and in his prologue to *Cligés* he mentions having adapted parts of Ovid's *Metamorphoses* (his *Philomena* is extant) and a version of the Tristan legend, which has not been preserved. See Norris J. Lacy and Joan Tasker Grimbert, eds, *A Companion to Chrétien de Troyes* (Cambridge, 2005).

[2] The Middle French period covers roughly the fourteenth through sixteenth centuries. See Christiane Marchello-Nizia, *Histoire de la langue française aux XIVe et XVe siècles* (Paris, 1979).

– more focused on the work of converting verse to prose – did not perceive a significant difference between the language of their models and their own; this awareness emerged later, after the turn of the sixteenth century.[3]

At the court of the dukes of Burgundy, in particular, a number of epics and romances were 'translated' from verse to prose, including Chrétien's first two works, *Erec et Enide* and *Cligés*. Both of these romances were prepared in the context of the court of Philip the Good, who ruled over Burgundy from 1419 to 1464. The prose *Erec* was composed between 1450 and 1460;[4] the prose *Cligés* is dated 1454 [NS 1455].[5] We now have two fine critical editions of these romances that we owe to Maria Colombo Timelli.[6] These prose romances have much in common, but the theory of an identical author, proposed early on, has now been abandoned; while it is true that the two adapters exploit many of the same themes, a stylistic and formal analysis of their prose reveals considerable divergence.[7]

Although both romances were penned during Philip's reign, it is not certain that the duke actually commissioned them, nor is there any proof that he even read or appreciated them.[8] But we do know that he was passionate about Arthurian literature in all its forms, as were his forebears, Philip the Bold and John the Fearless. Indeed, the public for whom late French Arthurian romances were destined avidly consumed these works. Their popularity – and the nostalgia for the Round Table and for Arthur as a model sovereign – can be explained by a number of factors: the ubiquitous state of warfare that characterized France in the late Middle Ages; the creation of chivalric societies on the part of the nobility, which was struggling to retain its power; and the flowering of regional courts and the rise of urban centers, two phe-

---

[3] See her 'Mémoire linguistique dans les réécritures arthuriennes des XVᵉ et XVIᵉ siècles', Colloque 'Temps et mémoire dans la littérature arthurienne' (Bucharest, May 2010). Forthcoming.

[4] Not to be confused with a prose interpolation featuring Erec found in Paris, Bibliothèque nationale de France (henceforth BnF) fr. 112, a fifteenth-century *Lancelot-Grail* manuscript prepared for Jacques d'Armagnac, and BnF fr. 12599. In this series of Erec's adventures, which has little to do with Chrétien's story, the episodes are interlaced with others in the prose *Lancelot*; the edition by Cedric E. Pickford (*Erec, roman arthurien en prose publié d'après le MS fr. 112 de la Bibliothèque Nationale*, 2nd edn, rev. [Geneva, 1968]) detaches them from this context and assembles them to make a single story.

[5] The date of 1454 is Old Style (OS), that is, it follows the Julian calendar, which was replaced by the Gregorian calendar in 1582; this New Style (NS), which is still used, calculates the number of days between equinoxes more precisely and affects the dating of earlier documents.

[6] *L'Histoire d'Erec en prose: roman du XVᵉ siècle* (Geneva, 2000) and *Le Livre de Alixandre Empereur de Constentinoble et de Cligés son filz: roman en prose du XVᵉ siècle* (Geneva, 2004).

[7] See Colombo Timelli's linguistic and stylistic analysis of this question in '*Erec* et *Cligés* en prose: quelques repères pour une comparaison', *Le Moyen Français*, 51/52/53 (2002–2003), pp. 159–75. See also the extensive note devoted to this question by Catherine Deschepper, 'De l'adultère comme résistance à l'empereur usurpateur... La convergence des intrigues amoureuses et politiques dans le *Cligés* en prose', in *La Littérature de la cour de Bourgogne, Actualités et perspectives de recherche*, ed. Claude Thiry and Tania Van Hemelryck, *Le Moyen Français*, 57/58 (2005–2006), pp. 67–86 at 71 n. 15).

[8] The author dedicates the prose *Cligés* to 'mon treshault et redoubté prince' (my most lofty and feared prince), who was probably Philip, but we can only speculate about the reception that the romances enjoyed at the Burgundian court. (See 'Reception' below.)

nomena that increased the reading public. Late French romance, which can be loosely defined as texts written, rewritten, or prepared by scribes and early printers from the fourteenth to the early sixteenth centuries, played an important role in the development and evolution of Arthurian materials and the perpetuation of Arthurian ideals.

The fifteenth century constitutes a central moment in this period; it is at this time that the court of Burgundy, especially under Philip the Good, reached its zenith, rivaling that of the king of France in power, splendor, and patronage. Philip's Burgundian state included not only present-day Burgundy and the Franche-Comté ('the two Burgundies'), but also a good part of what is now Belgium, Holland, Luxembourg, and northern France – Artois, Flanders, Hainault, Holland, Zeeland, Brabant, Limburg, Lothier, Namur, Luxembourg – the major urban centers being Dijon, Lille, Brussels, Bruges, and Ghent.[9] These extensive holdings resulted from power and territorial struggles that took place over the course of the fourteenth and fifteenth centuries; Philip the Good continued to rely on the strategies used by his father and grandfather, John the Fearless and Philip the Bold, which included marriages and tactical alliances as well as armed conflicts.

War was a constant of daily life for nobles, burghers, and commoners of the time. Long sieges were frequent, more important in many ways than pitched battles. For their armed conflicts, the dukes relied on the most sophisticated weaponry, and Philip the Good, in particular, assembled an impressive store of artillery.[10] Playing at war was also an important part of this lifestyle: *pas d'armes*, jousts, and tournaments were often organized for entertainment; they were also a means of displaying prowess and power. The duke himself was a great jouster, an activity he enjoyed even more than hunting and falconry.[11]

Marriages were a particularly important moment to mark, and a tourney was therefore usually held at such a time. Philip the Good's third marriage, to Isabel of Portugal, in 1430, was just such a moment. Not only was this an occasion for spectacular pageantry, but Philip also created at the wedding feast the Order of the Golden Fleece. Reminiscent of the Knights of the Round Table (like the Order of the Garter, its English counterpart), Philip's Order met in solemn assembly once a year. At its inception it numbered twenty-four knights, chosen at first among the nobility from Philip's holdings, then from different territories. The Order was a political instrument

---

[9] Richard Vaughan details the geographic boundaries in *Valois Burgundy* (London, 1975), pp. 23–5. See also his *Philip the Good: The Apogee of Burgundy* (London, 1970; new edn: Woodbridge, 2002).

[10] Robert Douglas Smith and Kelly DeVries, *The Artillery of the Dukes of Burgundy 1363–1477* (Woodbridge, 2005), pp. 23–33, 85–136.

[11] On these recreations, see especially Vaughan, *Philip the Good*, pp. 145–9; but consult also Richard Barber and Juliet Barker, *Tournaments. Jousts, Chivalry and Pageants in the Middle Ages* (New York, 1989).

meant to increase Philip's prestige and demonstrate his sovereign power. Its statutes reposed on religious and chivalric principles.[12]

Burgundy was known not only for its political and military might but also for its flourishing culture. Philip the Good presided over one of the most splendid courts in Europe; he gave extravagant banquets featuring elaborate 'entremets' – table decorations and exhibits that included huge 'props' (e.g., castles), and tableaux or theatrical spectacles.[13] Contemporaries who lived at the court evoke at length its sumptuous elegance and prestige.[14] Courtly etiquette and protocol were strictly defined; however, lest we equate these aspects with total refinement, it is useful to recall that not only was Philip a womanizer (he had some eighteen illegitimate children), but also the ducal chamber was the locus of male bonding through licentious jokes and stories.[15]

Not all of Philip's entertainment was of this sort. Music, literature, and art had their place. Philip was the foremost art patron of his period, employing for a time the celebrated Jan Van Eyck as his official court painter and *valet de chambre*. A great bibliophile, the duke had a very impressive library and managed to increase fourfold the 250-book collection that he had inherited. As he was particularly fond of illustrated books, he formed groups of scribes and illuminators to produce them. He also maintained writers and chroniclers at his court and possessed an unusual number of chivalric epics and romances. Not only did he collect the works of earlier authors, like Chrétien de Troyes (he owned the manuscript BnF fr. 12560, containing *Yvain*, *Lancelot*, and *Cligés*); he also bought and commissioned many works, including entirely new ones, as well as prose versions of existing verse works.[16]

The court of Burgundy was thus a preeminent political, military, and cultural center in the fourteenth and fifteenth centuries. Georges Doutrepont's landmark studies underscore the importance of this court in the production of late medieval works, and in particular of the *mises en prose*.[17] Without this

---

[12] Vaughan, *Philip the Good*, p. 57; Bertrand Schnerb, *L'État bourguignon 1363–1477* (Paris, 1999), pp. 295–304.

[13] Vaughan, *Philip the Good*, pp. 56–7 and 142–5; Schnerb, pp. 322–8; Otto Cartellieri, *The Court of Burgundy* (New York, 1929).

[14] In *Philip the Good*, Vaughan cites several of these descriptions, including a letter written by one J. De Pleine, a minor player at the ducal court (pp. 144–5), and a passage from Jaques Duclerq's *Mémoires* (p. 348). See also Schnerb, pp. 319–37.

[15] Schnerb, pp. 285–9.

[16] On BnF fr. 12560, see Patrick de Winter, *La Bibliothèque de Philippe le hardi, duc de Bourgogne (1364–1404)* (Paris, 1985), pp. 250–1, and Roger Middleton, 'Index of Former Owners', in *Les Manuscrits de Chrétien de Troyes / The Manuscripts of Chrétien de Troyes*, ed. Keith Busby, et al., 2 vols (Amsterdam, 1993), II, pp. 87–176 at 104–7, 128–9. This thirteenth-century manuscript was inherited from Margaret of Flanders, Philip the Bold's wife. The purchases and commissions are discussed by Schnerb, pp. 346–58; see also Georges Doutrepont (cited below).

[17] Georges Doutrepont, *La Littérature française à la cour des ducs de Bourgogne; Philippe le Hardi, Jean sans Peur, Philippe le Bon, Charles le Téméraire* (1909; rpt Geneva, 1970) and *Les Mises en prose des épopées et des romans chevaleresques du XIVe au XVIᵉ siècle* (1939; rpt Geneva, 1970). On the dukes' patronage, see also Roger Sherman Loomis and Laura Alandis Hibbard Loomis, *Arthurian Legends in Medieval Art* (New York, 1938), p. 125.

indispensable socio-political and cultural context it is impossible to grasp the nature and significance of the two fifteenth-century prose renderings of Chrétien's first two romances that we are presenting here in modern English translation for the first time. If we have decided to publish them together in a single volume it is because, though undoubtedly the work of two different adapters, they have much in common: both are prose adaptations of romances by Chrétien; both were written for the Burgundian court in the mid-fifteenth century; and both are relatively short works, often considered together by the few critics who have studied them.

Translation as 'transmutation'

The authors of the prose reworkings of Chrétien's romances were not simply translators. They appropriated his texts in a number of ways, one of the most evident being the omission of his name. While this choice may indicate a lack of interest in Chrétien himself, as Colombo Timelli states,[18] it is above all part of a process of appropriation similar to the one that Chrétien himself used with his sources, be they oral or written. Typical of this kind of annexation is the inclusion of the *Charrette* in the thirteenth-century prose *Lancelot*: the prose writer had no compunction about 'lifting' Chrétien's text and rewriting it to fit into the new context, as authorship did not carry the same sense of originality, ownership, and rights as it does today.

As part of this act of appropriation, the prosifiers eliminated Chrétien's prologue and rewrote their own, in each case presenting their work as a 'transmutation' of rhyme into prose. The choice of this term (the verb 'transmuer' is the form it takes in the texts) suggests the wide-ranging nature of the modifications the adapters make; the final products are in fact reinventions of Chrétien's romances. While the prose texts respect the general outline of the original plot, the transformations affect every aspect: language, style, content. Many of the changes can be attributed to 'acculturation'. Jane H. M. Taylor borrows this term from anthropology to characterize a particular type of rewriting; she defines it as 'a process whereby the socio-culturally unfamiliar is recast in familiar terms, so that the reader can understand systems and phenomena in a source text as corresponding to his own ideologies, preconceptions and behaviour patterns'.[19] Taylor points out that the changes are sometimes so small that they at first seem unimportant; by studying even 'minor' details, it is possible to gain insights into the culture for which the new text was written. Other types of adaptation concern what one might call 'literary style' and language.[20] There is often overlap among these 'categories'; in a great number of cases the meaning is affected.

[18] Introduction to *Erec*, pp. 18–19; introduction to *Cligés*, pp. 11–12.
[19] In an important article, 'The Significance of the Insignificant: Reading Reception in the Burgundian prose Cligès', *Fifteenth-Century Studies*, 24 (1998), pp.183–97 at 183.
[20] Linguistic changes are studied by Colombo Timelli in the introductions to her editions: *Erec*,

The specific techniques used by the prose authors are familiar to readers of prose Arthurian works: abbreviation, amplification, and rationalization. The process is complex, as one or more methods can be combined, so that individual episodes are modified in various ways: some sections may be abridged or omitted, while others are lengthened; new episodes may be invented. At the same time, the prose rationalizes or clarifies events that were ambiguous in Chrétien, and it introduces new rhetorical flourishes, while suppressing those found in the verse. It is in fact a total 'remake'; the process might be compared to that of a seamstress who takes in hand a wedding dress passed down from grandmother to daughter to grandchild, refitting and redesigning it to conform to the needs and tastes of its most recent owner.

As the following discussion will show, it is often difficult to separate the different types of changes from one another; they are intertwined. Our discussion will center first on modifications concerning above all the content: Erec's motivation in departing on his quest; the ending of the romances; the expansion of military actions; and the reduction of the lovers' monologues in *Cligés*. We will then turn to several techniques of adaptation focused on 'literary style': the use of direct discourse, description, and authorial interventions.

In both romances the prose redactor makes adjustments to the plot. In *Erec*, the prose version clarifies motivation: it is clear that the hero's goal in the central section is to test Enide; furthermore, when Erec falls to the ground and Enide thinks he is dead, the prose suggests that he is feigning death, thus emphasizing his motivation. A striking change is operated on the end of both prose texts. In Chrétien's *Cligés* the conclusion reveals that as a result of Fenice's successful ruse, empresses were henceforth imprisoned, implying that the heroine came to be seen as a negative exemplum, the very fate she had hoped to avoid. The prose writer omits this ending and substitutes his own: Cligés and Fenice live happily ever after and have many children; at their death their oldest son becomes emperor in legal succession. The author of the prose *Erec* concludes the romance in a similar fashion: the two endings are so close that it almost seems as if one were copied after the other. Both demonstrate a concern with legal succession as well as closure.[21]

One of the tendencies of late romance is an emphasis on warfare, often to the detriment of amorous developments. It is the consensus that this is the case for our two prose texts.[22] In the first part of Chrétien's *Cligés*, the

---

pp. 25–37; *Cligés*, pp. 49–57.

[21] The writer of the prose *Cligés* probably did not use the Chrétien manuscript that was in the duke's collection and has come down to us (C; BnF fr. 12560, as mentioned above), but it may be based on a manuscript from the same group. Catherine Deschepper points out that both C and R (BnF fr. 1420 – a manuscript very close to C) are missing Chrétien's ending (p. 77 n. 19).

[22] See Norris J. Lacy, 'Arthurian Burgundy: The Politics of Arthur', in 'Late Medieval Arthurian Literature', in *The Arthur of the French. The Arthurian Legend in Medieval French and Occitan Literature*, ed. Glyn S. Burgess and Karen Pratt (Cardiff, 2006), p. 496.

siege of Windsor Castle is described in some detail, and it is notable that the prose expands this section significantly, introducing contemporary artillery.[23] In the prose *Erec*, the tournaments and jousts are reported at length, despite the narrator's assurances of brevity,[24] and the author even adds a tourney just before the end, after the coronation of the royal couple, perhaps reflecting Philip the Good's analogous manner of marking significant occasions.

While it is true that both prose authors amplify passages on military prowess, it would seem that the love plot is still of considerable interest. The women (Soredamors, Fenice, and Enide) are well-developed characters. Although the elaborate monologues in *Cligés* are shortened and simplified, Fenice's emotions, in particular, are explored in various other ways, as in her extended conversations with Thessala, in which she focuses on Alix's usurpation of Cligés's rights in order to justify her refusal to share her body with her husband.[25] The prose author also develops the character of the duke of Saxony, transforming him into a lovesick suitor and a worthy rival for Alix and Cligés.[26] In *Erec* the prose actually augments the passages containing Enide's complaints, adding personifications such as Love and Despair that exteriorize her inner feelings. Personifications are also added in *Cligés*, most notably in the development on Maternal Love in chapter 2, when Thantalis laments Alixandre's departure for Arthur's court.[27] But the most striking addition to the prose *Cligés* regarding the love intrigue is that of a totally new episode (chapter 53), in which the hero comes upon a maiden who has taken refuge in the forest in order to avoid a forced marriage to a man she does not love; recognizing the analogy with Fenice's situation, Cligés resolves to hurry back to Constantinople.[28]

The introduction of personifications noted above is part of a series of transformations in literary style that affect the use of direct discourse, de-

---

[23] Colombo Timelli, introduction to *Cligés*, p. 171. The various weapons used in this siege reflect the importance of gunpowder artillery at this time. Of the four Valois dukes, Philip the Good is best known for having 'strengthened both numerically and in its overall power and diversity' the impressive gunpowder weaponry train that he inherited from his father. See Smith and DeVries, *The Artillery of the Dukes of Burgundy*, p. 85.

[24] A full list of such statements is provided by Jonna Kjaer in 'Les complaintes d'Enide dans l'*Histoire d'Erec en prose*, roman bourguignon', in *'Contez me tout': Mélanges de langue et de littérature médiévales offerts à Herman Braet*, ed. Catherine Bel, Pascale Dumont, and Franck Willaert (Leuven, 2006), pp. 243–58 at 246–9. The tournament after Erec and Enide's wedding, for example, takes up more space than in Chrétien. The redactors recast completely the jousts and tourneys.

[25] See Deschepper, pp. 73–4.

[26] See Joan Tasker Grimbert, 'Love and War in the 15th-Century Burgundian Prose *Cligés*: The Duke of Saxony's Passion for Fenice', in *War and Peace: New Perspectives in European History and Literature, 700–1800*, ed. Nadia Margolis and Albrecht Classen (Berlin, forthcoming).

[27] Colombo Timelli, introduction to *Erec*, pp. 40–4; Kjaer, pp. 250–4. See also the discussion of Rebecca Dixon's research on personification in the section on 'Reception' below.

[28] Colombo Timelli, introduction to *Cligés*, pp. 37–8, and '*Talanz li prant que il s'an aille*: le v. 5056 du *Cligés* de Chrétien de Troyes et l'invention d'un prosateur du XVe siècle', in *Favola, mito e altri saggi. Studi di letteratura e filologia in onore di Gianni Mombello* (Alessandria, 2004), pp. 359–75. For further analysis of the episode's function, see Joan Tasker Grimbert, 'The Fifteenth-Century Prose *Cligés*: Better Than Just Cutting to the Chase', *Arthuriana*, 18.3 (2008), pp. 62–72.

scription, and authorial intervention. Sometimes dialogue is removed. Critics have pointed out that at the moment of crisis, Erec's response to Enide's explanation for her tears is eliminated, resulting in a change in Erec's motivation: he no longer admits that his detractors are right about his lack of prowess, as he does in Chrétien.[29] Sometimes the dialogues are shortened so that the action moves along more quickly: when the vain lord attempts to seduce Enide, the exchange between the two actors is abbreviated, but the passage is also modified so that the lord appears much more traitorous and Enide much more loyal toward her husband. However, there are occasional moments when narrative is turned into dialogue. In the *Erec*, for example, when the couple spends a night in the forest, Erec tells Enide to sleep while he watches; she refuses, and he lies down to sleep. Chrétien's narrative is brief, with no dialogue, whereas the prose text actually provides description absent in the verse and transposes the exchange between Erec and Enide to dialogue form, thus dramatizing the moment. Similarly, in *Cligés* the narration of the decision and arrangements for Fenice's feigned death and removal to a secluded spot, which are made more rapidly than in Chrétien, are rendered in direct discourse.[30] The *Cligés* adapter also adds or augments many passages of solemnized mourning, with elegies and laments voiced by Alix, Cligés, and the townspeople.[31] A particularly striking change in *Cligés* is the adapter's transformation of Fenice's simple request for an orchard into an emotional hymn to the springtime renewal of Nature.[32]

Other ways in which the prose authors rewrite their texts are by abridging descriptions or omitting them altogether. Both of our adapters provide very abbreviated accounts of wedding and coronation festivities. Portraits, too, are shortened: the *Erec* adapter condenses the description of Enide when she first appears, while the *Cligés* adapter omits Alixandre's 100-line comparison of Soredamors's head and body to a pinioned arrow in a quiver.[33] Among the most significant cuts in the *Erec* are the portrayals of the hero's clothes and armor; the absence of these representations, along with a continued emphasis on Enide's clothing, suggests a modification in the focus of the romance.[34] On the other hand, as we have just seen, our authors sometimes amplify descriptions. In the prose *Cligés*, the redactor describes in remarkable detail Jehan's tower and orchard where the lovers take refuge after Fenice's supposed demise (see 'Reception', below). He also elaborates on the gruesome punishment – quartering – that is meted out by King Arthur to the four traitors captured by Alixandre at Windsor Castle. His strongly

[29] See Colombo Timelli, introduction to *Erec*, pp. 40–1.
[30] See Deschepper, pp. 74–5.
[31] See Martha Wallen, 'The Art of Adaptation in the Fifteenth-Century *Erec et Enide* and *Cligès*', diss. University of Wisconsin, 1972, pp. 294–5. Wallen suggests that these passages show how important funereal art was in Philip's court.
[32] See Wallen, pp. 231–2; Colombo Timelli, introduction to *Cligés*, pp. 34–6.
[33] Wallen, p. 256.
[34] See Carol J. Chase, 'The Devil is in the Details: Enide's Clothes in the Burgundian Prose *Erec*', paper presented at the 44th International Congress on Medieval Studies, The Medieval Institute of Western Michigan University, Kalamazoo, MI, May 2009; article forthcoming.

developed sense of right and wrong explains why he takes pleasure as well in adding details that paint Alix as a totally despicable character and in caricaturing the doctors from Salerno as old, ugly, lascivious men.[35]

Authorial interventions[36] are also the object of significant changes. As many scholars have noted, the ambiguous and ironic comments found in Chrétien's works have for the most part disappeared. Instead, we find more developed comments on transitions from one narrative thread to the next, much like those in the interlaced narratives of the great prose cycles; remarks signaling brevity (e.g., the determination to refrain from describing at length certain scenes, such as the wedding feasts in *Erec* and *Cligés*);[37] and examples of 'epic address' during battle scenes (invitations to the listener or reader to participate vicariously in a battle).[38]

The modifications made by the prose writers are thus multivalent; they are so numerous and varied that the new texts are indeed 'transmutations'. As we explain in the next section, early critics were quick to judge that these prose rewritings were mediocre, that the translations were clumsy adaptations or flat summaries of Chrétien's masterpieces, and, hence, devoid of any literary interest. However, close examination of the way the prose authors approached their task leads to an appreciation of their craftsmanship: like the late fifteenth-century illuminator who painted over earlier miniatures in a manuscript of the *Lancelot-Grail* that had belonged to the duke of Berry in order to bring them up to date, these authors attempted to make Chrétien's works interesting to their contemporaries.[39]

The reception of the prose *Erec* and *Cligés*

We do not know how our romances were received at the Burgundian court in the mid-fifteenth century.[40] It is curious, though, that in the sixteenth and

---

[35] Wallen, pp. 335–41, 347–8.

[36] We do not attempt to distinguish between author and narrator here; a finely argued presentation of the problems this distinction raises in a medieval work is provided by Roberta L. Krueger, 'The Author's Voice: Narrators, Audiences, and the Problem of Interpretation', in *The Legacy of Chrétien de Troyes*, ed. Norris J. Lacy, *et al.*, 2 vols (Amsterdam, 1987), I, pp. 115–40 at 115–18.

[37] In the *Erec* one of these remarks on brevity is accompanied by a suggestion that a long description is unnecessary because the reader knows very well the nature of the festivities (p. 211).

[38] Martine Thiry-Stassin has studied this aspect of *Cligés*: 'Interventions d'auteur dans le *Cligés* en prose de 1454', in *Hommage au professeur Maurice Delbouille*, special issue of *Marche romane* (1973), pp. 269–77; see also Kjaer, pp. 245–50, and Colombo Timelli, introduction to *Cligés*, pp. 25–6. Though the interventions may be more frequent in *Cligés* than in *Erec*, their nature is similar in the two romances.

[39] BnF fr. 117–20, inherited by Jacques d'Armagnac from his grandfather, the duke of Berry; Jacques had many of the miniatures overpainted.

[40] See Colombo Timelli's nuanced remarks in her introductions to *Erec*, pp. 21–3, and to *Cligés*, pp. 12–13. Kjaer argues that the *Erec* may not have appealed to the duke because it presented a sympathetic picture of Enide's situation at a time (1454) when he was having serious conflicts with his wife, Isabella of Portugal; see pp. 243–4.

seventeenth centuries we find no traces of the adventures of *Erec* and *Cligés* in either verse or prose. Pierre Sala, who produced a *Chevalier au lion* (1522) and a *Tristan*[41] (between 1525 and 1529), showed no interest in our protagonists, and titles referring to them are not to be found in the Bibliothèque Bleue, which in the seventeenth century began producing inexpensive books (including many romances) for the masses. It was not until the second half of the eighteenth century that excerpts of Chrétien's *Erec et Enide* and *Cligés* were published in the Bibliothèque Universelle de Romans.[42]

The prose renditions of *Erec* and *Cligés* first came to the notice of scholars at the end of the nineteenth century when Wendelin Foerster published them as appendices to his editions of Chrétien de Troyes's verse texts.[43] They were long ignored, however, for two reasons. First, as more modern editions of Chrétien's works appeared – and indeed proliferated – scholars no longer consulted Foerster. His editions of the two prose texts, which were not only buried in the appendices of his editions of Chrétien's romances but also printed in a smaller font, more or less disappeared from view. Second, the few scholars who examined the prose versions deemed them inferior to their models; rather than reading them as products of their time, they compared them to the works of Chrétien, the recognized master of Arthurian romance. Gaston Paris, in his first review of Foerster's edition of *Cligés*, characterized the prose as 'très médiocre'.[44] Foerster himself had emitted an even harsher opinion, calling it a tasteless and totally worthless dilution and mutilation of the Old French text (p. xxvii).

One of the first to examine the prose romances as works in their own right was Georges Doutrepont, author of two seminal books, the first on the literature of the Burgundian court and the second on the genre of the *mises en proses*.[45] He believed they had a twofold interest: he appreciated them for the information they could provide, first, on works that were no longer extant and, second, on the history and culture of fifteenth-century France, especially the duchy of Burgundy. In his eyes, then, their value was solely informative, not literary. Calling them a kind of 'free translation', he did find some merit in the structural and stylistic changes introduced by the redactors.

Although Doutrepont's assessment was hardly glowing, we must credit him with anticipating the subsequent, much more fertile, stage of criticism when scholars would begin to evaluate these works in the context of their epoch and their public. If they were not yet willing to recognize their literary merit, they did acknowledge that the prose authors had made remarkable

---

[41] Modern editors have called this work both *Tristan* and *Tristan et Lancelot*.

[42] See Colombo Timelli, introduction to *Cligés*, p. 13.

[43] Christian von Troyes, *Sämtliche erhaltene Werke*, ed. Wendelin Foerster. Halle: vol. I, *Cligés* (1884), prose *Cligés*, pp. 281–338; vol. III, *Erec et Enide* (1890), prose *Erec*, pp. 253–94.

[44] Gaston Paris, '*Cligès*', éd. Foerster, *Romania*, 13 (1884), p. 446. In his review of *Erec et Énide*, Paris totally ignored the prose rendition; '*Erec et Énide*', éd. Foerster, *Romania*, 20 (1891), pp. 148–66.

[45] *La Littérature française à la cour des Ducs de Bourgogne* and *Les mises en proses*.

efforts in adapting Chrétien's romances to cater to the tastes and interests of their contemporary audiences.

Among the first studies devoted to the process of adaptation were two quite different dissertations written in the early 1970s by Martha Wallen and Bette Lou Bakelaar.[46] Noting the omission, alteration, and even invention of various episodes and countless details, Wallen argued that the adapters skilfully reinterpreted their source and systematically varied the text in order to convey a particular meaning. She showed how they 'corrected' what they saw as faults of logic and motivation in the source.[47] Moreover, she stated that many changes were plainly designed to clarify aspects of the earlier romances that Chrétien had left ambiguous, such as Erec's testing of Enide, or to provide a more rational causality, such as the precautions taken by the lovers and their accomplices in *Cligés* to make sure the plots they concocted would evade suspicion.[48] Other changes were made to please the intended patron or audience; for example, the modernization of – or increased emphasis on – combat tactics and weaponry and the abridgment of passages highlighting love casuistry and extolling 'courtly' virtues like *largesse*. For Wallen the prose *Cligés* was a document of political flattery, and most of the changes made to glorify the hero were meant to provide a model or *miroir* for the dukes of Burgundy.[49] As for *Erec*, she concluded that the prose author was critical of Enide, whereas Erec was exonerated of any fault.[50]

Bakelaar, who learned of Wallen's dissertation as she was beginning her own, purposely concentrated on different aspects of the prose romances, such as literary influence, misogyny, and didacticism. She concluded that the prose authors had treated the male protagonists more sympathetically than the women, endowing them with moral qualities that made them models of conduct for members of Philip's court. She devoted an entire chapter to a comparison of the prose *Erec* and the prose *Cligés* (based on results gleaned from a computer-generated concordance), in which she focused on syntactic and stylistic matters, with a view to discovering if the two works had a common author; she concluded that it was possible, even probable, a view that today's critics do not share.[51] Around the same time as Wallen's and Bakelaar's dissertations were completed, Martine Thiry-Stassin contributed a study on authorial intervention in the *Cligés*[52] that anticipated Maria

---

[46] Wallen, 'Art of Adaptation' (1972); Bette Lou Bakelaar, 'From Verse to Prose: A Study of the 15th-Century Versions of Chrestien's *Erec* and *Cligès*', diss. Ohio State University, 1973.

[47] See in particular chapters 2, 3, and 7; Wallen published chapter 3 as the article 'Significant Variations in the Burgundian Prose Version of *Erec et Enide*', *Medium Ævum*, 51 (1982), pp. 187–96.

[48] Wallen, 'Art of Adaptation', pp. 35–6 and 218–21.

[49] Recently, Catherine Deschepper has examined this hypothesis and rejected it. See pp. 84–6.

[50] Norris Lacy dissents from this point of view; see below.

[51] This chapter is summarized in her article, 'Certain Characteristics of Syntax and Style in the 15th-Century *mises en proses* of Chrestien's *Erec* and *Cligès*', *Semasia*, 3 (1976), pp. 61–73. See Colombo Timelli's critique of her method and conclusions in '*Erec et Cligés* en prose: quelques repères pour une comparaison', esp.161–2.

[52] See n. 38 above.

Colombo-Timelli's large body of critical work on technical aspects of the romances (see below).

Following the lead of these pioneering studies, Norris J. Lacy and Jane H. M. Taylor published in the 1980s and 1990s a number of important studies that underscored the extent to which our two prose romances were products of their time.[53] Lacy showed how the prose *Erec* approaches the central enigma of the motivation of the two main characters and the nature and function of the testing sequence. Pointing out that Erec's motivation is clarified in the prose, he observed that Enide's is more complex: her fault is compensated by the narrator's unreserved praise. Lacy concluded somewhat paradoxically that 'the prose text offers not a psychological study but a sort of manual of wifely conduct'; in the testing sequence, Enide 'proved herself the equal of Griselda'.[54] Lacy dissents from Wallen's assertion that the prose adapter 'sided with Erec', as does Jonna Kjaer, who has suggested that the emphasis on Enide's lamentations shows that the prosifier allowed her to play a much more independent and important role.[55]

In a later article devoted this time to the prose *Cligés*, Lacy analyzed the way in which the author, 'more interested in focusing on the external obstacles in love than in dramatizing inner conflicts about it', condensed the dialogues and monologues of the two sets of lovers for an audience that he assumed would have found them 'tedious', thinking they would have little patience with the intricate casuistry that dominates the love intrigues in Chrétien's romance. He also noted the absence of irony, particularly in the treatment of the romance's ending (as discussed in the previous section).[56] Lacy's studies brought these two romances to critical attention, and his discussion of some of the important adaptations made in the prose romances has contributed to our understanding of the texts. His judgment – less indulgent than Wallen's and Bakelaar's – that the redactors were mediocre writers who would clearly 'not be mistaken for Chrétien de Troyes'[57] reflects the context of the time, one in which critics were only beginning to study late romance and appreciate it.

As mentioned earlier, Jane Taylor, who was one of the first scholars to appreciate the later romances, contributed in 1998 a remarkable study demonstrating the value of considering the phenomenon of 'acculturation'.[58] Her analysis of two episodes, one from *Erec* and the other from *Cligés*, is rich

---

[53] This same concern was already present in Wallen's dissertation; see especially her chapter 5, 'The New Esthetic of the Burgundian Court'.

[54] Norris J. Lacy, 'Motivation and Method in the Burgundian *Erec*', in *Conjonctures: Medieval Studies in Honor of Douglas Kelly*, ed. Keith Busby and Norris J. Lacy (Amsterdam, 1994), pp. 271–80 at 279–80. On Enide's assimilation to Patient Griselda, see Charity Cannon Willard, 'Chrétien de Troyes, Burgundian Adaptations of', in *The New Arthurian Encyclopedia*, ed. Norris J. Lacy *et al.* (New York, 1996), pp. 91–2 at 91.

[55] Lacy, p. 277 n. 13, citing Wallen, 'Art of Adaptation', p. 62; Kjaer, p. 249.

[56] Norris J. Lacy, 'Adaptation as Reception: the Burgundian *Cligés*', *Fifteenth-Century Studies*, 24 (1998), pp.198–207. Passage above quoted from p. 200.

[57] *Ibid.*, p. 205.

[58] See n. 19 above and the definition in the previous section.

in its implications for further work on the two romances. Examining the presentation of royal authority in the episode of the hunt of the stag and the bestowal of the kiss in *Erec*, Taylor concludes that 'the prose text assimilates the mysterious or the ironic political systems of Arthur's court to a model that would have been comfortably comprehensible to a Burgundian audience – a model in which the ruler's choices, the ruler's edicts, are primary and incontrovertible' (190). Her analysis of *Cligés* focuses on the prosifier's extraordinarily detailed expansion of Chrétien's description of Jehan's tower and orchard as a particularly notable instance of adaptation to the Burgundian court's tastes for sumptuous and extravagant objects. For example, the 'estuves' (baths) of the verse text become in the prose 'a riot of sophisticated plumbing, with porphyry fountains, birds and beasts gushing water from their beaks and mouths, little streams, tubs and baths and pools'. This description seems to reflect the dukes' fascination with water and hydraulics as seen in their estate at Hesdin and in the water-borne 'entremets' at their feasts. As Taylor notes, it is significant as well that the prose author takes care to explain how Jehan managed to finance the labor and raw materials needed to build such a splendid dwelling (pp. 185–6).[59]

Maria Colombo Timelli belongs to the same 'generation' of scholars who, like Lacy and Taylor, focused renewed scholarly attention on the prose renditions of Chrétien's romances. In her first studies, she concentrated on technical aspects of the romances at a time when she was preparing her most important contribution, her outstanding critical editions of the prose *Erec* (2000) and the prose *Cligés* (2004), which have not only served as the basis for the translations in this book but have also provided us with a wealth of valuable information for each romance – an extensive introduction including a survey of previous scholarship and a linguistic analysis, useful notes that often compare the prose to the verse version, an unusually complete glossary, and a detailed bibliography. As our own bibliography shows, Colombo Timelli has contributed a large number of studies focusing on aspects of these romances that are revealing of various techniques of adaptation and modernization used by the prose writers. She has also investigated in some detail a number of linguistic and stylistic questions, many of which are summarized in the introductions of her editions.

We can measure the progress made in the past several decades in our understanding and appreciation of the prose *Erec* and the prose *Cligés* by comparing the dissertations of Bakelaar and Wallen with the more recent one (2003) by Catherine Deschepper. Its title alone, '"Mise en prose" et "translation". La traduction intralinguale des romans de Chrétien de Troyes en moyen français', testifies to the sophistication of the approach, as does the article that the author published concurrently, in which she presents an ad-

---

[59] Colombo Timelli mentions three other examples of this same sensitivity to the economic aspects of a project (introduction to *Cligés*, pp. 41–2). Wallen had discerned a similar concern in several places in *Erec* (e.g., Erec assures a squire who offers him food that he will be paid for his generosity); see 'Art of Adaptation', pp. 53–4.

mirably rigorous thematic and stylistic analysis of the way the prose author 'legitimized' Fenice's adultery by linking it explicitly to Alix's usurpation of the rights of his brother and his nephew.[60] Rebecca Dixon, for her part, takes a different approach, showing how the adapter of the prose *Cligés* developed Chrétien's personification of love – and its distancing effect – to justify a love that some readers might have condemned. (By virtue of her marriage to Alix and given the importance of the relation to the maternal uncle, Fenice's love for Cligés could have been considered incestuous.)[61] Another example of how subtle the comparison of the prose romances with their models has become is Michelle Szkilnik's fine study on the reworking of the siege of Windsor Castle in the prose *Cligés*. She details the various changes made by the author to depict Alixandre as an imposing, authoritative leader of the type that his audience would more readily recognize than the character as originally drawn by Chrétien.[62]

As we have shown, the Burgundian prose versions of Chrétien's romances have begun to attract more appreciative audiences, but the impression remains that their literary value is slight. Although a few studies, such as those by Jonna Kjaer, Joan Grimbert, and Carol Chase, have attempted to change that critical commonplace,[63] too many scholars are quick to judge them as Charity Cannon Willard did when she reiterated the harsh opinion of earlier scholars, stating that the *Cligés*, 'without the charm of Chrétien's style and especially without the analyses of love, seems faded'.[64] This impulse is understandable, for surely the most disconcerting result of the prosification of Chrétien's romances is the elimination of many of the Champenois poet's comic and ironic touches celebrated by so many scholars writing in the wake of Peter Haidu's pioneering study on aesthetic distance in *Cligés* and *Perceval*.[65] It is the loss of those touches that has too often left the impression that the prose versions are flat, unengaging, and somehow deficient, that the art of storytelling has given way to simple textual summary. It may be hard to argue with the general assessment that in the prose, the stories of Erec and Enide, and of Alixandre and Soredamors and Cligés and Fenice, lose much of the piquancy that Chrétien scholars prize in the originals. Nevertheless,

---

[60] Thèse de doctorat (Louvain-la Neuve, 2003); 'De l'adultère comme résistance à l'empereur usurpateur...'. (Unfortunately, Deschepper's thesis was unavailable for consultation.)

[61] 'The Wedding Reception: Rewriting the Ideological Challenge in the prose *Cligès* (1454)', *Cahiers de Recherches Médiévales*, 24 (2007), pp. 315–26.

[62] 'Le prince et le félon: Le siège de Guinesores dans le *Cligès* de Chrétien et dans la prose bourguignonne', *Cahiers de recherches médiévales*, 24 (2007), pp. 61–74. See also her excellent survey, 'Medieval Translations and Adaptations of Chrétien's Works', in Lacy and Grimbert, eds, *Companion to Chrétien de Troyes*, pp. 202–13, esp. 209–11.

[63] Kjaer (see the discussion in the previous section). Grimbert, 'Better Than Just Cutting to the Chase' and 'Love and War in the 15th-Century Burgundian Prose *Cligès*'; both of these articles reveal the art with which the prose author treated the love intrigue. Chase, 'The Devil is in the Details'.

[64] 'The Misfortunes of *Cligès* at the Court of Burgundy', in *Arturus Rex*, ed. W. Van Hoecke, G. Tournoy, and W. Verbeke, 2 vols (Leuven, 1991), II, 397–403 at 403.

[65] *Æsthetic Distance in Chrétien de Troyes: Irony and Comedy in 'Cligès' and 'Perceval'* (Geneva, 1968).

we believe – and hope to demonstrate by publishing these translations – that each of the anonymous redactors demonstrates considerable skill in identifying the elements that he or she finds most important and attractive and in fusing them into renditions that are generally very readable, sometimes compelling, often clever, and in places quite charming.

Manuscripts[66]

As a number of critics have remarked, many of the prose rewritings of verse romances survive in a single manuscript. This is the case for the prose *Cligés*, which has come down to us in a modest paper volume now held in Leipzig, in the Universitätsbibliothek (Rep.II.108). Dated March 26, 1454 (= 1455) in the explicit, the manuscript is listed in the inventory of books in the library of Philip the Good that was prepared in 1467–8 after the duke's death. The text is divided into 'chapters' preceded by red rubrics, three of which were not completed. Space was left for nine illustrations, all to be placed after a chapter end, just above the rubric announcing a new chapter. The function of the rubrics is to announce the main features of the narrative that occur in each section; taken together, they summarize the intrigue and allow the reader to locate passages.[67]

Colombo Timelli points out that a number of elements connect this manuscript with the one in which the prose *Erec* is preserved complete, Brussels, Bibliothèque Royale 7235 (B), an undated paper volume that figures in the same inventory of the duke's books as that of the prose *Cligés*. The binding, format, paper, and filigrane are similar. Thus, like its 'brother', the text of the prose *Erec* is also divided into chapters preceded by red rubrics, but there are no illustrations, and none were intended (no spaces have been left for them). The manuscript was probably prepared between 1450 and 1460.

The opening section of the narrative of the *Erec* has also been conserved in a second, longer version in Paris, BnF fr. 363 (P). This text appears in the last tome of a magnificent six-volume manuscript containing a compilation known as *Guiron le Courtois*, prepared c. 1470 for Louis de Bruges. The portion of the *Erec* that is interpolated into *Guiron* comprises what Chrétien

---

[66] In the introductions to the prose *Erec* and *Cligés*, Colombo Timelli provides a complete description of the manuscripts (*Erec*, pp. 9–15; *Cligés*, pp. 7–11).

[67] Fifteenth-century *mises en prose* are characterized by this segmentation of the narration; the rubrics, which are often found in manuscripts from the fourteenth century on, can be seen as an early form of chapter titles. See Danielle Quéruel, 'La naissance des titres: rubriques, enluminures et chapitres dans les mises en prose du XVe siècle', in *À plus d'un titre. Les titres des œuvres dans la littérature française du Moyen Age au XXe siècle* (Lyon, 2001), pp. 49–60; and Colombo Timelli, 'Pour une "défense et illustration" des titres de chapitre: analyse d'un corpus de romans mis en prose au XVe siècle', in *Du roman courtois au roman baroque*, ed. Emmanuel Bury and Francine Mora (Paris, 2004), pp. 209–32. In this article Colombo Timelli points out that the titles can also guide the interpretation, but they can be misleading too when they fail to mention important events described in the chapter (pp. 211, 216).

called 'le premerain vers', which relates the opening hunt for the stag and the sparrow hawk episode, but it also includes Erec and Enide's wedding and the tournament that follows, ending with the festivities upon their arrival at the court of Erec's father, King Lac. Colombo Timelli presents the text of this manuscript on pages facing those of MS B in her edition of the *Erec*.

A third manuscript, Oxford, Bodleian Library, Douce 383 (O; c. 1480–1500, owned by Engelbert of Nassau), probably transmitted a similar version of the *Guiron* compilation. The Oxford manuscript contains 17 folios that were removed from two luxuriously illustrated volumes (each folio consists of a fragment of text with a magnificent illumination). The cover illustration of our book reproduces a detail from the page comprising a segment of the prose *Erec* (fol. 15 in the present MS; fol. 142 in the original). The miniature, placed above a rubric in red announcing the tournament held after Erec and Enide's wedding, shows two knights (Erec and Gauvain) jousting, observed by ladies in a gallery and others standing outside. In an appendix to her edition, Colombo Timelli has edited the text of this folio, which is very close to that of MS P.[68]

Medieval manuscripts did not have a title page; there were titles on the spine or the cover of the binding, but since the original binding did not always survive, this designation may reflect later reception of the text rather than the name given by the author. Even in the case of bindings that have come down to us, this title, which is very often the name(s) of the main protagonist(s), was undoubtedly provided by the person who did the binding or the one in charge of conserving and classifying the books of a patron such as Philip the Good. Indeed, the preparation of a manuscript was usually divided up among different artisans: the scribe, the rubricator, the illuminator, and the binder. How much control an author had over the actual form of his work once it was passed to these specialists is thus questionable.[69] For these reasons, scholars turn to the prologues that almost always opened a text for information regarding authorship, patron, audience, and title. Thus, though the spine of manuscript B of the prose *Erec* carries gold letters that mark it as 'EREC' (this may be the original binding), we need to examine other evidence.

Surprisingly, the inventory done right after the death of Philip the Good lists the first words of the prologue as the 'title'.[70] It is therefore the prologue that provides the most useful information. While Chrétien titled his

---

[68] As Colombo Timelli points out, we know nothing about the genesis of the Burgundian *Erec* (introduction to *Erec*, p. 16). In her study of the relationship between the three manuscripts, Colombo Timelli concludes that they have a common source in an archetype, α, but that MSS P and O descend from a 'sub-archetype', γ, for they have a number of lessons that differ from those in B but resemble Chrétien's text (introduction to *Erec*, pp. 49–66; conclusion, with a stemma, on p. 66).

[69] A good overview of these issues is provided in the essays in *Histoire de l'édition française*, ed. Roger Chartier and Henri-Jean Martin, vol. I: 'Le livre conquérant. Du Moyen Age au milieu du XVIIᵉ siècle' (Paris, 2nd edn 1989).

[70] Cited by Colombo Timelli, introduction to *Erec*, p. 1 n. 2. As is frequent in inventories from this period, the books in the duke's collection are identified by a physical description and

first romance *Erec et Enide* – thus focusing on both husband and wife – the prose author clearly thought of his romance as 'The Story of Erec, son of King Lac', a designation that occurs not only in the prologue but also in the rubric that immediately follows and serves as an incipit in the one complete manuscript (B). Should we conclude, along with Colombo Timelli, who takes into consideration the rubrics as well as the title, that Enide is 'nearly systematically effaced … in the places where the function is to highlight the essential elements of the work', confirming that the prose work consists of an 'anti-Enide reading of Chrétien's romance', and that the transformations operated by the prose author center the story on Erec, thus imposing a title focused uniquely on the male protagonist?[71] Or should we agree with Jonna Kjaer, who argues that Enide is not absent from the rubrics nor is the text dominated by Erec, and that therefore the title should carry both names (p. 258)? Our choice for the title is based on different considerations: we have used that found in the prologue. It reflects the way Erec presents himself in the text, emphasizing his lineage and his status as a king's son.

The prose *Cligés* also modifies the title that is usually given to Chrétien's work. Although neither the verse nor the prose prologue contains a title, the explicit in Paris, BnF fr. 794, the manuscript penned by Guiot, refers to the text as *Cligés*. In his prologue Chrétien states that this new story is about a young man from Greece who is a relative of Arthur, adding, however, that before anything is recounted about him, the life of his father will be told. Cligés, who is unnamed at this point, has pride of place in this bipartite tale. This double focus is clearly articulated in the prose version: the incipit (in red; printed in italics in Colombo Timelli's edition and our translation) presents the romance as the story of the noble and valiant emperor Cligés, which is recounted in two parts. The first is devoted to Cligés's father, Alixandre; the second, to Cligés, son of Soredamors. As in Chrétien, Cligés is clearly at center stage; it is noteworthy that he is foregrounded as Soredamors's son. Colombo Timelli's title, *Le Livre de Alixandre Empereur de Constentinoble et de Cligés son filz*, is that found on a parchment label on the cover of the binding. Protected beneath a 'kind of miniature picture frame' made of transparent horn held in place by copper strips or surrounds, it probably dates from the time when the manuscript was prepared.[72] This title reflects the bipartite organization of the romance. Like that given to the *Erec*, it ignores the women who play a prominent role in the romance and focuses on

---

a 'title', which may be that appearing on the binding or the first words on the first and/or second folio or page.

[71] Introduction to *Erec*, pp. 33–4 (our translation; Colombo Timelli concurs here with Wallen's hypothesis that the adapter is critical of Enide). As Colombo Timelli herself notes in 'Pour une "défense et illustration" des titres de chapitre', it is impossible to know who composed the chapter titles; they may very well be the work of the planner of the manuscript.

[72] Colombo Timelli, introduction to *Cligés*, p. 1, describes the label; it is of a type commonly found during this period. The quote is taken from David Pearson, *Provenance Research in Book History: a Handbook* (London, 1994). The inventory prepared shortly after Philip's death, in 1467–8, gives a short title, 'Le Livre de Alexandre, empereur de Constantinoble', cited by Colombo Timelli, p. 1.

the male protagonists; however, the absence of the women characters in the title is not as striking as in the case of the *Erec*, since Chrétien's romance is not entitled 'Cligés and Fenice'. In any case, it is likely that the prose *Cligés* was 'baptized' by the binder or the duke's 'librarian', his treasurer, who was responsible for the care of his books.[73]

---

[73] Schnerb, p. 347.

Translators' Notes

Our goal in translating these two romances has been to provide an attractive and readable text that conveys as much as possible the flavor of the original. We have therefore retained most of the traits that are part of their alterity, all of which are common to medieval narrative. In the manuscripts, sentences tend to 'run on'. Each moment of the narrative is linked in various ways: by connectors such as 'and', 'then', 'upon hearing that', 'at that moment', or by repeating an action: 'he grabbed his sword' is often followed by 'once it is seized …' While we have lightened the narrative by suppressing some of the constant recurrences of 'and', we have kept most of these connectives.

Since punctuation was minimal in manuscripts, one of the decisions editors must make is where to place commas, semi-colons, periods, and even paragraph breaks. As translators, we have made more frequent sentence breaks (and many more paragraph breaks) than Colombo Timelli has done in her editions. The syntax of the original is occasionally so tortured that we have had to resort to changing the order of the dependent clauses. Old and Middle French tend to use personal pronouns 'loosely', the referent often being located quite far from the pronoun. (This structure is particularly characteristic of the long passages devoted to jousts.) Where necessary, we have clarified by replacing a pronoun with a proper noun or some other element describing the referent, such as 'the opponent'.

One of the most striking characteristics of French writing in general is the frequent use of the historical present tense. Medieval narrative constantly switches back and forth between the simple past tense and the historical present. Since this incessant alternation does not translate well into English, we have generally used the past tense, reserving the historical present chiefly for passages describing an exceptionally dramatic moment. Another constant in medieval narration is the use of synonymic doubling, using two words that mean nearly the same thing, such as 'strike' and 'hit'. Where possible, we have reproduced this stylistic feature of the original texts. Double negatives are also frequent, and we have occasionally maintained this construction as long as the meaning was clear.

In order to preserve the flavor of the original, we have also retained some of the proper nouns in their French form, rather than turning them into English. Thus, we have kept Erec, Cligés, Alix, Alixandre, Gauvain (rather than Gawain), Perceval le Gallois (instead of Perceval the Welshman), and Guivret le Petit. However, since Guenièvre, Artus, and Keu are forms that may be disconcerting in English, we have preferred Guenevere, Arthur, and

Kay; and for the long lists of knights' names in *Erec*, we have used English translations.

One of the challenges of translating these romances has been to render technical terms in English; as noted above, armed conflict in all its forms plays an important role, and the prose authors have updated the tourneys, jousts, and battles to reflect the evolution of practices as well as the use of artillery and other specialized equipment. The new versions also refer to various aspects of the cultural context in which they were written that may be unfamiliar to the reader. A glossary of medieval terms, found at the end of our book, is intended to fill that gap.

For both texts, the manuscripts divide the narrative into unnumbered chapters, each of which is preceded by a rubric in red. In our translations, as in Colombo Timelli's editions, these rubrics appear in italics, with a chapter number. Page numbers referring to her editions are placed in square brackets.

Our translation of the two romances is based on the Leipzig and Brussels manuscripts, using Maria Colombo Timelli's critical editions. For the *Cligés*, lacunae (which are identified in the footnotes of our translations) have been filled by referring to Foerster's critical apparatus and Colombo Timelli's notes. In the case of the *Erec*, the Paris manuscript constitutes an additional resource.

JTG & CJC

THE STORY OF EREC, SON OF KING LAC

Translated by Carol J. Chase

Contents

The Story of Erec, Son of King Lac

[p. 101] It is possible to profit greatly in various ways through the constant practice of the telling of stories containing the deeds of nobles who lived long ago. Because I have been presented with the rhymed story[1] of Erec, the son of King Lac, I shall, God willing, devote a little time to transposing it from verse into prose in the way that follows below; and I pray those who will read it to excuse my rough style.

[p. 103] 1. *Here follows the story of the noble and valorous knight Erec, and this first chapter recounts how King Arthur decided to go hunt the white stag in the forest full of adventures*[2]

The present tale begins this way: one day at Easter King Arthur, whose glorious renown extended throughout the world, held court at Cardigan Castle, assembling, may God be my witness, many noble barons, for more kings, dukes, princes, counts, lords, and knights were present than he had ever brought together for a day. You must not ask if ladies and damsels[3] of high and noble lineage were present: there were more than five hundred, and you should be aware that it was a noble thing to see their social station. Our account will not stop to speak about the dances, tourneys, and other entertainments; rather, in order to get to the heart of the matter right away, it will start off by saying that at this time, when King Arthur was at Cardigan, nearby in the forest of adventures there was a stag totally different from all the others because it was completely white. Several times it had been the object of a hunt, and the king had issued an edict in order to bestir his barons: whoever took the stag could, without prejudice and at his choosing, have a kiss from the most beautiful lady or girl at court. Thus it came about that, before the festivities were over, since there were many knights on hand, King Arthur planned to go into the forest of adventures to hunt the stag. Sir

---

[1] 'Histoire' in the French, which can be translated as 'history' or 'story'. The adapter seems to distinguish between 'histoire' and 'compte', in general using the first to refer to the source and the second for his own tale. In order to retain the difference, I have translated 'histoire' as 'story' and 'compte' as 'account' or 'tale'.

[2] A literal translation would be 'adventurous forest', which would include the connotation of risk inherent in the French.

[3] 'Damoiselle': term used for unmarried women; in order to avoid over-using the word 'damsel', I have translated this word in various ways: damsel, young woman, young lady, girl. I have reserved the word 'maiden' for 'pucele', a term that suggests the young woman is a virgin.

Gauvain tried to dissuade him from this object, saying that it could cause very great harm, for each and every lady and damsel had a husband, father, brother, or male friend who would try to forbid the kiss if she were the one to be chosen. To which the king responded that there was to be no debate, stating, 'May it please God, I will keep my word and pledge, [p. 105] as it befits a king to do!' These words silenced Sir Gauvain.

The king had the hunt announced for that afternoon, and there was not a single knight who did not prepare himself to appear for it. At the appropriate hour the king, attired nobly, mounted his horse. He sounded his horn so that his knights would follow suit, and soon all were ready to set forth. Seeing this, the king spurred forward confidently and was already far ahead when the queen, having obtained the king's permission to go to the sporting event, mounted a white palfrey and followed, along with several ladies and girls. With the queen there was a noble knight named Erec, the son of King Lac, at that time a young man who daily grew more handsome, wise, and strong. The queen's party moved fairly quickly; however, no sooner had they entered the forest than the stag was off, because the huntsmen had stirred it with their hounds, and the other dogs were barking loudly as they chased it. Out in front of all the other knights, King Arthur followed the stag, which was already excited by the hunt and dangerous to confront. Though she could not see anything, the queen listened avidly to the sounds of the chase. Finally she lingered in the shade of a pine tree. As soon as she had pulled aside, she saw from afar an armed knight on horseback. Lance in hand, shield hanging from around his neck, and sword at his side, he was leading closely, at his right, a young lady with a proud dwarf, who was holding a knotted whip and riding a steed that he guided and controlled skillfully.

[p. 107] 2. How a maiden and Erec were struck by a dwarf

Having noticed the knight and young woman, Queen Guenevere wanted to know who they were and where they were from, so she ordered one of her damsels[4] to go tell them to come speak to her. Quick to obey the queen's command, the young lady set forth, upon which the dwarf, who saw her, moved forward to meet her, questioning, 'Miss, who's chasing you? Don't come any farther! You have no business here.'

'Yes, I do indeed,' replied the maiden, 'for the queen has sent me to speak to the knight who is your master.' The dwarf said she would not pass, but the damsel ignored him and was trying to continue on her way when the traitorous dwarf set upon her and struck her hand so hard with his whip that it left a purple mark, which made her very unhappy. Upon her return, she began to cry softly; the queen, seeing that she was wounded, turned

---

[4] The passage is faulty: 'who they were and where they were from' are repeated here; corrected following Colombo Timelli's note, p. 213.

to Erec and said, 'Ah, my dear knight, how might vengeance be taken on the evil, proud knight who, through his outrageous behavior, allowed my maiden to be hurt? Go to the knight and tell him he must give the dwarf his just deserts, or I will take care to remedy this insult if I can find out who he is.'

Not wishing to disobey the queen's orders, Erec headed towards the dwarf, who came forward to stop him, saying, 'Vassal, get out of here! There's nothing here for you, and I suggest you leave, or you will regret it!' Not deigning to respond but rather acting courageously, Erec attempted to spur forward. But then the dwarf approached and, knowing his master was armed while Erec was not, hit him so hard in the neck with his whip that he nearly drew blood. This action displeased Erec deeply, but he dared not strike back because he knew he would be blamed if he beat a dwarf that he could kill with one blow. And since he saw the armed knight proudly watching him, ready to set upon him if he struck the dwarf in his presence, he said to himself that it would be senseless to avenge himself, so without a word he turned back [p. 109] and told the queen what had happened. The queen was upset, but hardly had she finished commiserating with her knight, Erec, than she saw the other knight set off on his way on a high road.

Erec said he would follow him and as soon as God had provided him with armor – hauberk, helmet, lance, and shield – he would fight the proud knight and take vengeance for the offense he had done to him and the damsel, if Fortune were on his side. The adieux were tender. The queen prayed that her knight might have good fortune. And Erec set out in pursuit. May God watch over him!

We will leave him in order to speak of King Arthur, who took the stag and returned to Cardigan in great honor. The queen told him about Erec's adventure, asking him not to take the kiss until her knight had returned. The king agreed, and so we will return at once to speak about Erec, who was skillfully pursuing the knight with the dwarf and young lady.

[p. 111] 3. *How Erec was given hospitality by a host who had a beautiful daughter of noble lineage but who was poor*

Erec therefore constantly kept the knight in view, until he found himself at a well-situated castle where there were a number of knights and squires calling in sparrow hawks, tercels, goshawks, and falcons.[5] The inhabitants of the castle saw the armed knight arrive, so they came to meet him, showing him great honor and making joyous demonstrations of friendship. They led him to lodgings in the castle. When Erec saw these events, he passed through the gate, and found a knight of high rank, an old man, aged and nobly attired, whom he asked where he might find lodgings. And the knight

---

[5]   See the glossary for these and other terms pertaining to medieval culture.

replied that in his house he would be well served, if he pleased. Erec, who asked for nothing better, thanked him warmly.

The knight led him to his home, and there Erec dismounted from his horse, which was well taken care of. And shortly after Erec's arrival the mistress and lady of the house appeared with her beautiful daughter. This young woman, the knight's daughter, was the most beautiful of all the women in the world, even though she was poorly attired, for Nature had placed in her enough beauty for a thousand! And our present story testifies that everyone marveled at how Nature could have imagined such a perfect masterpiece in a maiden's body. To speak of her beauty, Yseult the Blond's hair was nothing compared to the mane with which the young lady was adorned. Her white skin, like a lily with the hue of a newly opened rose, was very fine. Her eyes were lovely and pleasant to behold. She had been endowed with such a mouth, nose, forehead, chin, and entire face that it seemed she had been made to be gazed upon, as the one whose beauty surpassed in every way that of the female sex. When this maiden of such a high rank saw Erec, the noble [p. 113] knight, she began to feel embarrassed and blush, because she had never seen such a handsome man, for the tale says his beauty could be compared to that of Absalom. It was the same for Erec when he saw this noble girl who, following the orders of her lord and father, the old knight, showed him into a hall beautifully decorated with numerous precious objects.

Finally suppertime approached, and water was brought for washing. Erec was invited by his host and lady to sup with them, for he seemed to them to come from a noble family. They were served, God knows, with great generosity. After supper, when Erec and his host entered into conversation, Erec asked him why his daughter was so simply attired, and he responded, stating, 'Alas, my friend, you know that poverty does ill to many, and this I can say through my own experience, for so help me God, I am very sad to see her so poorly dressed. But alas, I cannot do otherwise, for through the hazards of war and sea, I who was once a high and powerful landholder, am a very poor man in my present position. Despite my misfortune, there is no great knight in the surrounding lands who would not willingly take my daughter to be his wife. But when it pleases God, she will have something better, for because of her goodness and beauty, she merits having a king's son, a duke, or a great prince as a marriage partner. And though she is poor, she is no less noble; indeed, she is to be praised all the more than if she pretended to something more than her present state warrants.'

[p. 115] 4. *How Erec requested armor from his host*

When Erec heard his host's words, he esteemed and praised him in his heart, saying that he was blessed with fine qualities. He questioned him further, asking for information. He said, 'Sir knight, by your faith, I would like to know where all the knights I have seen in this castle come from. Upon my soul, it surprises me greatly.'

'Fair son,' the knight replied to Erec, 'I can tell you about this matter. They come from many places, and tomorrow there will be a festival that will take place in this way: following the custom that he has established, the count of Lalut, lord of this land, will give a sparrow hawk sitting on a silver perch to the knight who is accompanied by the most beautiful lady-friend.[6] In honor of her companion, she will go take the bird from its perch and bring it to him, unless someone raises an objection.'

'The ceremony is beautiful,' said Erec. 'But, dear host, if you know the name of the knight with white arms who entered the castle with a young woman and a dwarf a while ago, I beg you, tell me about him.'

'His name is unknown to me,' replied the knight, 'but I know him well by sight because he has carried off the sparrow hawk for two years in a row, and he will do so again tomorrow if no one stops him.'

'That would be too bad,' said Erec; 'he is hard and stubborn. May you know that if you thought I deserved it and wished to obtain armor for me, he would not carry it off without a battle with me.'

'Yes indeed,' said the aged knight, 'I am powerfully equipped in that regard.'

'By your grace, my lord,' said Erec, 'in addition to providing me with armor, please grant me another request.'

'May it please God,' responded the knight, 'I will not put myself in your bad graces by refusing another thing, provided it does not jeopardize my honor.'

'In order that you may know my condition,' said Erec, 'I assure you that I am the son of King Lac, Erec, so I entreat you, if I vanquish the knight [p. 117] mentioned earlier, may you allow your beautiful daughter to go take the sparrow hawk for me, and in my name. And if you are willing to grant me this pleasure, I promise you, upon my faith, that I will take her to my land and have her crowned queen, may God save me.'

The old knight was very joyful when he heard Erec say that he was the son of King Lac, for he had heard of his great renown over all the knights at the court of King Uterpendragon and King Arthur, so he said that he would be very distressed if he were the cause of his very dear daughter's not attaining such a high station. 'And so,' he said, 'I present my daughter to you and immediately give her to you in marriage, to take her away when you wish.'

Erec thanked his host, and God knows, there was great joy throughout the knight's house at the good fortune that they hoped would be due to the impoverished young woman.

---

[6]   The Middle French uses 'amie' here and elsewhere for the young women who accompany or are loved by knights; the word has a number of meanings, from 'friend' to 'beloved'. I have translated by 'lady-friend', 'lady-love', 'friend', or 'beloved'.

In reaction to this arrangement the noble maiden showed no emotion, for
her calm demeanor did not change at all. In her heart she was delighted,
and she responded so wisely to Erec's questions that he marveled at her
good sense and her gracious ways. At the end of the conversation, everyone
went to bed. Erec is in one bed, and the young lady is in another room, and
yet their two hearts are together, and Love had quite a lot to do all night,
advising the two lovers in whose hearts he had loosed his golden arrow so
deeply that they could not rest all night long. Several dreams of love kept
Erec and Enide awake throughout the night.

The next day, once dawn had broken, Erec got up, as did his host. They
dressed and went to church to hear Mass, as Erec was accustomed to serve
God first, before doing anything else. Once Mass was over, they returned to
their lodgings, and Erec asked for his harness, which was brought to him.
The maiden helped him put on his armor and placed a fine helmet on his
head. He girded his sword, then his charger was brought to him. He jumped
on without putting his foot in the stirrup and seized lance and shield. After
that the maiden, who was dressed according to the ability and power of her
father, was mounted on a palfrey. Then Erec set forth, the young lady at his
side. Everyone looked at them, especially at Erec, who was worth looking
at, for one could not see anyone more comely on a horse. People asked each
other who this was taking away the beautiful girl, but no one knew, so they
passed judgment and deposed according to the qualities they saw in the
knight's person – that he was good-looking, came from a noble family, and
that he was likely to carry off the sparrow hawk, for no one more handsome than he nor more beautiful than she could be assembled in one spot.
[p. 123] Erec and his lady-love did not stop until they arrived at the place
where the sparrow hawk was. When they reached the spot, Erec greeted
the ladies as best he could.

And the news reached the knight with the dwarf that a knight had arrived
who would have his beloved take the sparrow hawk if he did not gainsay
him. The knight responded that the other one would not carry it away and
that he knew of no knight in the world – no matter how good – against
whom he would not defend it. So he left his lodgings armed and on horseback, his lady-friend with him as well as his dwarf, and with a handsome
group he entered the area where his adversary was waiting.

The lord of the castle, the count of Lalut, came to see what was taking place
between the two knights and the ladies as well. And when the knight in

white armor came before the sparrow hawk, he addressed his lady-love, 'My beautiful young lady, who is so noble, for and in the name of my love, rightly will you go to take this sparrow hawk, which through your good graces, should belong to me, as it has the last two years. So prithee, in the sight of everyone, present it to me.'

Thereupon the young woman advanced to take the sparrow hawk, but immediately there was Erec, who said to her, 'Miss, go find a bird to amuse yourself with elsewhere, for this one is not for you! It is mine and belongs to the damsel you see here, who is incomparably more beautiful than you.'

The knight with the white armor was deeply troubled at hearing these words, but Erec took no account of his reaction. Instead, he had Enide, his lady-friend, come forward, and said, 'My noble miss, who surpasses all in feminine beauty, take this sparrow hawk that belongs more rightly to you than to anyone else. And if there is a man who wants to gainsay this, I will be happy to defend it in just combat.'

[p. 127] 7. *How Erec and the knight in white armor jousted together*

When the knight in white arms heard that Erec was offering to do battle, he went towards him very disdainfully and asked, 'Vassal, who are you to come challenge me for the sparrow hawk?'

'I am a knight from a foreign land,' said Erec, 'who, seeking the adventure I desire so much, has found it by saying that this sparrow hawk is mine.'

'You have never done a greater folly than to take on a combat against me,' said the white knight, 'for I have never found anyone, no matter how courageous he appeared, who dared to claim the sparrow hawk in my presence.'

'Unless I am convinced through armed combat,' said Erec, 'I cannot conceive that anyone other than my lady-friend might touch it, so if you have something to say, raise your index finger!' The knight did so, then distanced himself from his adversary, and after that, both of them spurred their chargers forward impetuously. And, as they were knights wishing to strike each other for love of their ladies, they pierced each others' shields, broke the saddle straps, and both fell so hard to the ground, with their horses on top of them, that they did not know where they were. Upon this encounter, even though they fell hard, there was no dishonor whatever, since the saddle straps had broken. They sprang to their feet with agility, and put their hands to their good swords. They approached each other, God knows, with a deep desire to vanquish each other, and in this way at the first charge, they both dealt such blows to each other that sparks flew from their helmets. Everything they reached was broken.

They strike over and over, covering themselves with their shields like the valiant champions they are – all this for love of their ladies. Because of the continuous rain of blows they are giving each other, helmets and, especially, shields are broken to pieces, and neither one of the two fails to pay for the battle with blood from his body. And they worked each other over so much that they no longer had the strength to strike as they had at the beginning. The maidens watched them, both of them crying in their hearts for their champions, [p. 129] who they saw were all bloody; and the two men, who were thoroughly exhausted, by mutual accord made peace until they could catch their breath and rest a little.

Erec sat in the field, which was verdant with abundant grass, then raised his head and, gazing at his beloved, his strength came back. He made an effort, and she opened her heart to him so that he felt no ache or pain; and then he remembered his promise to avenge Queen Guenevere's damsel against his cruel adversary, so he said to himself that he would give him many a sword-blow for the whiplash that the dwarf had given her. Anger renewed him, and suddenly, sword in hand, he addressed his enemy.

'Knight,' said Erec, 'I'm calling you back to combat, and it seems to me that we have rested enough for this time.' Then the knight got up and headed toward Erec, entering into combat once again, harder than ever, and during this skirmish, had Erec not been able to cover himself well with his shield, he would have been hurt several times; but God kept him safe. For no matter how many times the knight in white armor cut away a piece of his helmet, shield, or hauberk on the first attack, nevertheless he did not wound him to the quick. Harried thus, Erec did not fall prey to fear. He was intent on taking vengeance and, upon seeing his man exposed, he raised his sword and gave him such a blow on the side that he split open the hauberk and drove his sword so far into the knight's body that blood flowed freely.

[p. 133] 8. *How the knight was vanquished and surrendered to Erec, calling out for mercy*

Terribly fierce was the battle between the two knights. They struck and struck again, but each of them had a lion's heart for his lady, whom he saw present. Erec fought powerfully, and so did the knight. Neither one could gain anything on the other; rather, they tried each other out as equals. But among all the blows, Erec dealt one to his enemy that was so well served that it sundered his helmet and broke his iron coif so that he wounded him, bringing blood, without killing him. Feeling this blow, stunned, the knight staggered. Erec saw this, and putting his sword in its scabbard, he seized his enemy bodily and threw him to the ground. He took his opponent's sword from his hands, then unlaced his helmet and pulled it off far enough so that the knight's face appeared, bloodied and in a sorry state. And he would have already cut off his head because of the offense the dwarf had done in the forest of adventures, if the knight had not cried out for mercy, saying, 'Oh, sir knight, for God's sake, take pity on me! For if you killed me, you would not gather praise or honor, since I can no longer defend myself against you, and I never did anything against you personally that I can remember. So it seems to me that you have entered into mortal hatred against me for no reason; and finally, if I have harmed you, I beg your pardon.'

'So that you may know', said Erec, 'that it is not without a just and good reason that I want to kill you, I reply that I was the one who was with Queen Guenevere and her maiden yesterday in the forest when your proud and arrogant dwarf struck us with his knotted whip. Thus, very great blame should be imputed to you, who allowed a vile and abominable disfigured hunchback to strike the very pleasant young lady and me successively. You will swear to be my prisoner, or so help me God, I will take vengeance right now for your outrageous pride. And if you are willing to do as I say, I order you to go before night falls, along with your maiden and dwarf, to surrender to the queen and present my greetings to her, so that she may do with you what she pleases. But first, I must know what your name is, so that if you do not follow my orders, I will know who must be held accountable.'

The knight was completely overwhelmed when he heard Erec speak in this way. He responded [p. 135] that his name was Yder, the son of Nut, and that he was happy to go to the queen, and he gave Erec his word that he would do so. Erec had nothing more to say, so he let him depart after the preceding conversation.

[p. 137] 9. *How Yder surrendered to Queen Guenevere, who retained him as part of her retinue*

As soon as Yder had had his wounds bandaged, wishing to keep his promise, he mounted his horse; then in the company of his dwarf and the young woman, he followed the path until he arrived near Cardigan. At that moment Sir Gauvain and Kay the seneschal were at a window above the gate. They saw Yder approaching, so they pointed him out to each other, and the seneschal said it seemed to him that it was the knight the queen had talked about the day before.

'He could very well be the one,' said Sir Gauvain, 'since he's with a dwarf and a young lady, and his armor is quite damaged.'

After these words, by common agreement, they went to the queen and asked her, if she saw the dwarf who had angered her in the forest, would she recognize him. 'Yes, indeed,' replied Guenevere, 'but, upon your faith, why have you reminded me of it?'

'Because', said Kay, 'I saw a knight-errant armed from head to foot, and if my eyes can be believed, he's with a dwarf and a young woman.'

Thereupon the queen stood up and told the seneschal to take her to the spot from which he had seen the knight. The seneschal did so willingly. They set off, thinking to go to the window, but Yder had already entered the courtyard; therefore, they stopped to see his demeanor. When Yder saw he had arrived, as it is stated above, he dismounted, while Sir Gauvain advanced to help the young lady dismount; then the dwarf dismounted by himself. Yder asked for the queen, who had already called the king. He was led before them, and he headed where he saw the queen and fell at her feet. He greeted her as well as the king, then proceeded to say to the queen, 'To you, my very sovereign lady, I have been sent as a prisoner by a knight of noble birth who defeated me[7] today with the blade of his sword, in revenge for the injury that my dwarf did to [p. 139] your maiden yesterday. So we present ourselves to you, begging for mercy, and we are ready to make amends for our offense according to your good graces.'

'How is the knight?' asked Guenevere. 'Will he return shortly?'

'Certainly, my lady,' said Yder, 'when I left him, he told me that he would return here tomorrow, and may you know that he will bring with him the most noble damsel, indeed the most perfect, that anyone has ever seen.'

This response made the queen very happy, but she was nevertheless not silent. Instead, she asked the knight his name, his station, and the region he was from.

'My lady,' said the knight, 'it is right that I tell you all this. For my father, who was once in your service, was called Nut, and I, Yder, place myself at your service.'

On hearing these words, the queen prayed the king to take pity on the prisoner and release him, in exchange for being in her service for the rest of his days. The king was pleased, and Yder vowed to be loyal forever after.

But our tale will leave off speaking about the pledges of friendship that many knights made to him and will now turn to the deeds of Erec, who, after the departure of his prisoner, took hold of the sparrow hawk with great joy. The lord of the castle asked the beautiful maiden's father about Erec. He learned the truth and at once went to bow to him and present him with honor and service, indeed, inviting him to take lodging in his castle.

Erec thanked him heartily. 'But', he said, 'sir, forgive me; tonight I shall not leave my host, who has given me his noble daughter as my wife.'

'The gift is beautiful,' said the count of Lalut, lord of the land, 'for the maiden is perfect in beauty, goodness, refinement, and wisdom, and I am very happy about this great good that has come to her, for her mother is my sister. And since it pleases you to dine there with[8] my brother-in-law, my barons and knights and I will accompany you, if our company will please you.'

'Yes, indeed,' said Erec, 'when you arrive, you will be very welcome.'

[p. 143] 10. *How Erec arranged during supper to take Enide to King Arthur's court the next day*

Thus ended the conversation between Erec and the lord of the castle. Erec set out on the way to return to his host's home. Knights, ladies, and damsels escorted him. He dismounted, and at once knights and squires came forward

---

[7] 'Defeated me' inserted, as in MS P, to fill a lacuna.
[8] 'With' inserted from MS P.

to remove his armor. He was soon disarmed and dressed again; then he sat down at the table, the lord of the castle next to him on his left and his lady-friend at his right. After drinking and eating, he called his host and, smiling sweetly, said to him, 'Now, my host and father-in-law, you have given me the greatest pleasure in the world, and I thank you for it. May it please God, tomorrow I will take the beautiful maiden, your daughter Enide, with me to King Arthur's court, and I will show her the greatest honor that could come to her. I will take her as my wife and lady, as I should. And in a short time, if you please, I will send for you to go to my father's kingdom, where you will be received very joyfully, and upon your arrival, I will give you the city and castle of Roadam. And before three days have gone by, I will send you gold, silver, and lovely objects in great plenty.'

After this speech a young woman, Enide's cousin and close friend, and also a niece of the lord of the castle, came before her uncle, the lord, and said that he should be ashamed to allow Enide to be attired so poorly. To which he replied that she should give her cousin two or three dresses among the finest she possessed and that he would see to it that she had some new ones. The maiden said she would do so willingly. But Erec, learning something of these deliberations, replied to the girl that his beloved would not have a single dress; however, it was not through irritation, 'for', he said, 'I love her as much in her poor clothing as I would in richer things, and in this regard, I will let my sovereign lady[9] see to everything.'

'Well, then,' said the girl, 'I'll give her one of my palfreys, which are worth more than any others. And the one I will give her is black; it runs like a swallow flies and is as gentle as a lamb, so I prithee you may be pleased [p. 145] to accept it.'

'This is a gift I do not wish to refuse,' said Erec. The damsel sent for the horse, and soon a boy led it forward. Erec saw it and prized it, then he had it stabled in the same place as his steed, thanking the young woman profusely. The day was spent on many festivities, and the next day early in the morning Erec prepared to leave. And when Enide was ready, with the horses bridled and saddled, there came the lord of the castle, along with knights and ladies who arrived from everywhere to escort the maiden. Erec mounted his charger, while his friend got on her palfrey. They set out on their way and were accompanied quite far. When it came time to separate, once adieux and good-byes were said, the lord of the castle wished to send and dispatch some of his knights with Erec to escort and serve him, but Erec refused any company. And when the mother and father saw that their daughter must be led away according to the law of nature, they could not help crying. A hundred times over they kissed their beloved child, and at last they headed back, entrusting her to God's protection, while Erec continued on his way.

---

[9]   'Maistresse', a term that suggests that Erec considers Guenevere to have authority, to be an arbiter.

[p. 147] 11. *How Erec and Enide, his beloved, were joyfully received*
at King Arthur's court

All along the way Erec, the noble knight, could not keep himself from gazing at his beautiful, sweet friend, who for her part could not go without
casting her eyes on her own friend, through Love, who gave his consent. A
thousand times over Erec admired Enide's beauty, saying to himself that he
was fortunate indeed to have obtained the good graces of a maiden without
equal. Likewise, the girl was saying the same thing to herself, so that neither
one was defrauded, and the story says that never will laws or marriage unite
and join together in one desire two masterpieces of such outstanding beauty
and perfection.

Finally, at about three o'clock in the afternoon these two loyal lovers arrived at Cardigan, where everyone was standing about to watch them arrive.
At the windows of the castle were the king, the queen, Sir Gauvain, Perceval
le Gallois, and many other knights of the court. They perceived from afar Erec
and his beloved, and in great friendship they all went out together to meet
Erec; and even the king, who saw him approaching, went to greet him, as did
the queen. Words of welcome and greetings were not at all spared! Much was
made over Enide by the king, the queen, the ladies, and girls. The king took
her in his arms from her palfrey and led her in great honor up to the reception rooms in the castle. After them Erec and Guenevere followed, hand in
hand, and Erec began conversing[10] with the queen, stating, 'My lady, I bring to
you my beautiful friend, who is badly attired but is nonetheless from a noble
family, the daughter of a knight who is the brother of the count of Lalut[11] but
who through misfortune has lost his lands, income, and position. However, I
love her no less; indeed, I hold her as dear as if she were more richly attired.
Thank God, what she has is sufficient for me, and had I wished to let her be
more richly dressed, in truth, my lady, several noble ladies who are part of
her family would have gladly set to work at the task. But I did not allow it;
rather [p. 149] I have brought her to you in the condition in which she was
given to me, praying that you may do with her as you please.'

'Fear not,' replied the queen, 'as for love of you, I will do so much that
you will be very happy with me.'

[p. 151] 12. *How Enide was dressed in fine clothes*

Thereupon the queen went up to the beautiful young lady, Enide. She took
her white hand in hers, led her to her bedroom, then ordered that an outfit

---

[10] 'Conversing' inserted to fill a probable lacuna, as per Foerster's suggestion, p. 252, and
Colombo Timelli, p. 214.
[11] This statement contradicts the earlier indication that Enide is the daughter of the count's
sister.

that had been made earlier for her own use be brought to her, and a mantle as well. Her wishes were carried out. The maiden was undressed, down to her beautiful white chemise, then she was given a simple tunic. At the wrists it was adorned with beautiful gold embroidery worth more than a half mark and studded with stones: rubies, sapphires, emeralds, and diamonds. Over the tunic was placed a dress lined with ermine, then she was garbed with a mantle embroidered all over and trimmed abundantly, God knows how. After that two maidens came and put on her head a gold chaplet finely worked with every kind of flower that one could ask for. Beside all this, a splendid necklace was placed around her neck, and she was so well adorned that never before had a more beautiful lady been seen.

And for several reasons the queen took her immediately into her good graces, for in the first place, she was beautiful beyond all natural limits, and among one hundred thousand pleasing images, she was so perfect in every way that each and every one took pleasure in seeing her. Her sweet demeanor was confident and composed, and beyond that, she was so well brought up that it seemed as if she had spent her whole life at court and that she had been fashioned to serve as a model for others.

[p. 153] 13. *How Enide entered the hall, and the king*
had her sit beside him

After preparing the noble damsel Enide, the queen, who saw that she was completely ready, had never been so joyful. She left her chambers with the maiden, as well as ladies and damsels, then entered the hall where the king was. Upon seeing them arrive, the king rose to meet them. Likewise, all the knights honored deeply this very happy arrival of Enide. At that time there were present a great many knights of the Round Table, among whom our tale places Sir Gauvain, Lancelot du Lac, Gornemant, the Handsome Coward, the Ugly Hero, Melian de Lis, Malduis the Wise, Dodinel the Wildman, Hellis, Brien, Yvain the son of Brien, Yvain the Bastard, Yvain of the Moors, the Proud Knight, Yvain the son of Ameneuz, the Squire of the Golden Circle, Amanguis, Glangus, Tor the son of Arés, Girflet, Lohier the son of King Arthur, Sagramors the Unruly, Gerimons, and many more, all of whom marveled at seeing this young woman so well appointed with beauty and fine things. When the beautiful girl with the calm demeanor entered the room and saw so many high barons, it is not a wonder if she was embarrassed. She seemed passionately beautiful, and the king, who saw the light footstep and lovely walk of this noble young woman, took her by the hand and seated her next to him, in a more prestigious place than the queen, who, with her courteous manners, had him take this action.

[p. 155] 14. *How the king kissed Enide*

As soon as Enide had recovered her composure and was seated, the queen ventured to say to the king that, if he wished to choose the most beautiful woman at his court, he had hardly anything to do in order to take the kiss due to him because of the stag. Upon this reminder, the king sent for his close confidants and said that the maiden from the foreign land was more beautiful than any other. He asked each man's opinion. But, since they were able to adjudicate, it was quickly settled that she should have the honor of the stag and that the king could legitimately take the kiss without any prejudice, in order to keep his honor, his right, and to uphold his royal word. In conclusion, all debate having resulted in complete agreement, the king leaned down toward Enide and graciously took a kiss from her as the reward that was due to him because of the white stag he had killed. Humbly, Enide allowed the king to do so, in the presence of knights, ladies and girls, each of whom held her in high esteem.

Here our tale will leave off speaking of Enide's gracious demeanor for a little while and will now turn to say that Erec had five packhorses loaded with gold, silver, and great riches and sent them to his father-in-law and to his mother-in-law of Lalut, with ten knights and several servants and squires, who took the couple to the castle of Roadam, and in Erec's name had it announced that everyone should honor and obey them. Having accomplished this mission very well, the knights returned to Erec, their master, and told him how they had fared, which made Erec very happy. So he asked the king for permission to celebrate his wedding, and the king willingly granted it. He even sent word to the kings, dukes, counts, princes, and barons who were his vassals that, under pain of feeling his fury, no man, however brave he might be, should fail to be at his court at Pentecost. Once the announcements were made, there was not a single man who did not prepare to appear on the day named above.

First, we will speak briefly about those who came: Baldwin, count of Gloucester; the count of Divion; the count of the High Mountain; [p. 157] Count Godegrains; Maleus the baron; the lord of the Isle of Guerre; Guinganor, who was the male friend of Morgan the Fee; Aguichans, king of Scotland; his son Gondré; the fair king of Gomaret; Quernus, the king of Ariel; Billis, the king of the Antipodes; his brother Urien, who was a dwarf.[12] With him there were two other ugly and hunchbacked dwarves, the first of whom was named Gliogoro and the other, Gliogodolen. They were the object of many gazes, as they were smaller than any other dwarves, and they had large black faces with beards, and all their limbs were malformed.

---

[12] 'Who was a dwarf': Colombo Timelli signals, p. 214, that these words may be an error on the part of the scribe.

About the others who came – very numerous – our tale will remain silent in order to be brief.

The king knighted one hundred new knights, and on the predetermined day of Pentecost, the archbishop of Canterbury married the two lovers, Erec and Enide. Once the vows were taken, King Arthur, who was holding a round table for all comers, ordered the head butler to serve everyone who asked for food of any kind. Then he sat down at table with the queen; between them was Enide, the lovely bride, beautifully adorned with jewels and fine objects. Our tale will not mention the dishes, 'entremets', wine, or hippocras, for it would be too long to describe it all, and besides, each person can well imagine and consider that everything cannot be stated. We will not make a long account of the singers, harpists, drummers, minstrels, and skillful players of trumpets, buisines, bugles, and many other musical instruments. People danced, jousted, tourneyed, and the story states that all the instruments in the world were played on this high wedding day.

When evening came, because of her love for Enide and for Erec, the queen prepared Enide herself, and after advising her in several ways, had her get into bed. Thereupon Erec appeared, having already accompanied the king and the barons and the ladies until their parting. He entered the room, and when he saw his beloved lady, wishing to share in her much-desired company, he graciously took leave of the queen and remained there alone. He locked the door, and then [p. 159] his heart was filled with joy. He was overwhelmed, and before he was disrobed, Love had made him kiss and embrace a hundred times over his loyal lady-love. Finally, Erec undressed as quickly as he could, then as is the custom, filled with amorous bravery, he entered the maiden's arms. There they reached the summit of their desire; in both of them their hearts were filled with delight. Out of two hearts that can differ, Love made one alliance, and in great pleasure made them kiss, embrace, and hug each other a hundred thousand times. As for the remainder, our description remains silent, stating that in the heart of two lovers no greater love can be found. Thus, the next day the young lady was a woman, and when day appeared brightly and they had to get up, God knows they lamented; the night seemed too brief to them, and if it had lasted four times as long, they would not have been upset.

[p. 161] 15. *How the men of King Arthur's court held a tournament after the wedding*

Enide was greatly honored and very loving of her lord Erec: may God maintain them in their love! But no matter how good a horse is, it can stumble, as it will be said in what follows. Erec made many gifts and rich presents, and in honor of this important marriage, King Arthur held a round table for two weeks. Therefore, you can know well that the festivities that took place are not to be recounted or described. We will let the readers imagine all the countless activities there were.

And, to speak about Erec's deeds, our story recounts that the knights of the Round Table decided to hold a tournament that would take place two weeks after the wedding. Between Sir Gauvain on the one hand and Melis and Meliador on the other, the tournament was sworn, and they determined to hold it near Teneborc in a field that is still there. When came the day that the knights were to joust, lords from every region descended on the field in great pomp and set up so many tents, pavilions, and canopies worked with silk thread, cloth of gold, and every splendid thing that there was an infinite number, and it was a pleasure to see the pavilions sparkle in different ways in the joyous rays of the sun. Oh, what a lovely group of nobles were assembled in a single spot on the day predetermined by the marriage of the most beautiful woman in the world! Melis and Meliador set up their tents near the castle, and Sir Gauvain had his set up on the other side. In carriages and on lovely palfreys the ladies rode down there, and they said they had never seen such beautiful preparations and ceremonies for a tournament of a single day. They had all they could do, looking first one way and then the other.

And when it is time to take up their arms, the marshals of the tournament on both sides have the trumpets and high bugles sound until the field resounds with them. Then knights move out, taking up arms as elegantly as they can, with a good number of sleeves, [p. 163] pennants, and blazons on their helmets. The buglers have barely finished their call to arms when each and every one is mounted, armed with his shield, lance, helmet, and hauberk. On both sides the company of knights is handsome. They are eager to join in a melee, so they have the trumpets blown loudly.[13] And the good knights leap and spring and couch their lances, then meet with such abundant blows to the shields that one would not hear God thunder. Meliador and Melis accomplish beautiful feats of arms. Sagramors and Sir Gauvain do not lack courage. The knights snap lances, break shields, and knock men and horses to the ground in such a way that it is impossible to know which side has the better or the worse.

[p. 165] 16. *How Erec performed marvelous feats of arms*

All the lances had not yet been shattered when Erec, who was riding nobly behind the others, issued forth like someone who seeks only to acquire honor. He sat on a white charger, and the Proud Knight of the Moor, upon seeing him caper about, left the melee and went to meet up with Erec, who asked for nothing better. The horses were not spared, and when it came time to lower their lances, Erec struck the Proud Knight of the Moor in the middle of his shield with such a blow that he lifted his opponent out of the stirrups and boldly threw him to the ground, his legs in the air. Then the Proud Knight

---

[13] 'Loudly' supplied from MS P to fill a lacuna.

could say he had met his master at the lance, something to which he was not accustomed. Erec rode on, his lance raised, but before he could rush into the fray, there was Aguichans, the king of Scotland, who, striking and bashing repeatedly, came to joust with him. Erec looked, then immediately took on King Aguichans, and after breaking his reins and bit, he knocked him down, making him fall on the field.

After this blow, suddenly appeared the king of the Red City, who was a man of great nobility, and, like the valiant knights they were, the two of them charged each other so impetuously that the king of the Red City broke his lance against Erec's shield. And for his part, Erec shoved so hard against the king's person that the charger's saddle straps broke, and the king had no choice but to fall. Once these exploits were accomplished, Erec, with all the power of his shield, his own body, and his horse, flung himself into the thickest of the fray and made such an assault on a press of knights holding out on a hillock that he broke his lance; but before that, he struck down three of the best and strongest.

Then Erec put his hand to his sword and headed to the spot where he saw he could best employ himself, and he tested himself so much that those who saw him said indeed there was no knight more vigorous or harsh in the lists, for he performed marvelous feats of arms and undertook nothing that he did not carry through to the finish. On his part, Sir Gauvain, who wished to earn praise and honor, [p. 167] did not fail to exert himself. He struck and flung out at every attack in such a way that he knocked everyone down before him. He made several noble barons proceed on foot, with the help of Sagramors, Yvain, Girflet, and several others. They drove their adversaries up to the castle, right before the gate. There began, with renewed vigor, a new engagement.

Erec saw Sagramors exposing himself to risk, so he headed for him and with a well-aimed blow of his sword, greeted him so roughly that he stunned him and sent him to the ground. On the other side was Sir Gauvain; he saw Meliador and approached him, then he grabbed him by the helmet and with sheer strength, threw him to the ground and was ready to have him swear to be his prisoner when there appeared Erec, who ran to the rescue. With his shield, body, and horse, so powerfully did he run up against Sir Gauvain that neither of their horses had the strength to sustain the blows but had to fall, along with the knights. They jumped quickly to their feet, and they would already have tested each other with their swords if King Arthur, who did not want this encounter to take place, had not had retreat sounded. Because of that, they had to stop, and with equal honor going to one and the other, they separated and mounted their horses.

[p. 169] 17. *How Erec departed from King Arthur's court and went to his own land*

After everyone had ceased tourneying, the knights were soon out of their armor. Sir Gauvain, Sagramors, Melis, Meliador, and several others were the objects of conversation on the part of the king and the ladies. But of all the great feats of prowess that had been seen on one side and the other, it was judged that Erec had won and deserved the greatest triumph and praise. About the tournament our present tale will not speak any more.

Erec carried off the glory, and after everything was over, he took leave of the king, the queen, the ladies, barons, knights, and damsels, thanking them for their courteousness and the hospitality they had shown him as well as his lady, who knew very well how to thank each person. The king and queen were deeply saddened by the separation, though they gave their leave, urging the couple to return to see them as soon as they could. Once leave was obtained, having prepared his baggage, Erec and his handsome company of knights most regretfully departed.

He set out on his way, taking with him his dear lady, and did so well that at the end of six days he arrived near a well-situated city in which his father, King Lac, was staying. Before entering the castle of the city, he sent word to the king about his arrival. The king was very joyful and with his handsome retinue, promptly went to meet his beloved son Erec. At the meeting kisses were not spared. With great love the king received his son, then he saw the noble lady Enide. He bowed to her and she responded in kind. The king helped her dismount from her palfrey and with great honor kissed her, then led her up into his castle, which was well surrounded with gardens, rivers, meadows, woods, and other things fitting for a king's pleasure. And in the city, as a sign of this welcome, everyone celebrated: the streets were hung with silk cloths, rugs, and coverings; they were strewn with green foliage and fine grasses, and there was no one who did not praise God when they saw their young [p. 170] lord having as a marriage partner the most elegant lady in the world.

The lady was conducted to the church in order to give thanks to God. Once praises were rendered, everyone returned, and God knows what presents the nobles and commoners of the kingdom gave upon the occasion of the accession of this very noble lady. They gave her goblets, jugs, flacons, pots, pint mugs, gold and silver basins, fabric of every kind – silk, velvet, damask, satin, pourpre, and several other sorts – and if truth be told, no queen or princess could be more honored in her country than Enide was upon this first acquaintance. Among his other gifts, King Lac gave her numerous ladies, all of them happy to serve her and to be guided by her fine competence. But, neither more nor less than the sun surpasses in brightness the great splendor of the moon and the stars, likewise Enide surpassed the beauty of all the most attractive ladies and damsels who were assembled around her.

In this castle she lived for a long time with her beloved lord and husband, who fell in love with her so completely that he was always in her company, and with all his will, endeavored to serve, fear, and love her. Nor did Erec ever go hunting for game, or anywhere else, unless Enide was at all times with him. Enide conducted herself modestly with her husband Erec and, no matter how many traps were set for her through envy, there was never a ruse concocted through evil thoughts by a man or a woman that found a spot of baseness in her. For in being good, wise, devout, sober, generous with alms, fearing God, and watching well over her honor, she surpassed all other princesses. And therefore Nature would never have applied herself to form such a fine piece of work if she had not had divine power to help her compose it out of matter not corrupted by sin or malice. Thus Erec was so besotted with love that he forgot all about bearing arms, jousting, or tourneying, through which great harm arose for Enide, as will be told hereafter.

[p. 171] 18. *How Erec questioned Enide because she was crying, and she told him the cause of it*

Seeing Erec completely abandon the noble profession of arms in order to devote himself to the love of his wife, without whom he could not live or endure, the knights of the kingdom were very displeased, and they began to murmur about this true love, saying that Erec had become too childlike and that it did not bring him honor to neglect the exercise of knighthood in favor of the kisses and embraces he took daily from his love and lady. Nevertheless, no one dared to say anything to him, so they talked about it with the ladies, and through these ladies it became known to Enide, who was not happy about it. She was afraid that, if she alerted her lord, he might become angry with her. And for this reason, deeply uneasy, she carried in her heart these words touching upon her lover's honor.

The outcome was that one night among others, thinking about these remarks, she who did not want to be blamed or shamed, began to weep next to her husband, who, hearing his beloved's sobs and sighs, woke up and questioned her to learn the cause of her tears. Enide said she was not crying, but she was unable to find a way, upon her husband's supplication, to avoid telling him the truth, so she said to him, 'Ah, my lord, forgive me if I tell you something that you will not find pleasant. Upon my soul, all the knights and barons of this kingdom have not ceased murmuring against me for some time; they say in common that I'm corrupting you and that it is only because of me that you no longer exercise the noble art of arms. This dishonorable accusation grieves me deeply in my heart, and it is not without reason, for they all say that I'm holding you back, and that it is only because of me that you do not seek adventure in jousting and tourneying as well as you once did. And for this reason, I turn to God, for I would rather be dead than be the cause of hindering your honor and benefit.'

In reply to these remarks, Erec did not say a word; only, he decided to put to the test whether his wife Enide loved him loyally. But [p. 172] I do not say that suspicion and jealousy were the cause of this decision. Erec was very pensive, and he ordered Enide to prepare herself to set out on the road, telling her that he would go with her alone throughout the land to learn the craft of arms. To this Enide did not dare respond, but she was distraught. Erec got up and went off to make his preparations, and Enide remained in her chamber, weeping and speaking in this way.

19. *How Enide lamented about what she had said to Erec.*

'Alas! Miserable wretch, what have I done – I who have set my lord, who loved me so much, on a worrisome enterprise? Woe is me! What a great misfortune! God, what will become of me? I was too comfortable, enjoying too great an abundance of goods! Through good fortune I was elevated from the bottom, and now suddenly I must descend! Oh, evil mouth, procurer and administrator of this terrible mishap! This is a too sudden plunge that you have caused, lying in ambush against my happiness and noble position. Alas! Fortune had treated me too well, and I was too deeply honored when because of a sudden incitement to be truthful, I must certainly be exiled. The proverb that states that the goat scratches until it cannot lie comfortably is certainly true!'

Thereupon Enide prepared herself, then she had her palfrey saddled. And Erec entered a gallery and ordered that his arms be brought to him. He had a rug spread, on which they were laid out; he took his greaves, then put on the fine hauberk, girded the sword, and at this point hurried off[14] to take leave of the king, his father. The king asked him who would be going with him, and he replied, 'No one,' and that he wanted only his lady. The king said, 'It would be foolish to travel all alone through the land. Therefore, my advice is that you take with you the best knights here so that they may serve you [p. 173] in any need. Besides, it would be a great error for a king's son to travel all alone when he can do otherwise.'

Despite King Lac's remonstrations to his son, Erec held firm to his resolve and said that he would certainly carry out his voyage as he had determined, nor would anyone know where he intended to go. When the king heard these words, he did not know what else to say; rather, he let things be organized by his son, who set off in the company of his wife, with deep regrets, tears, and cries. When he reached the fields, he said to Enide that she must at all times ride out in front and that, as dearly as she loved him, she must keep from turning around, no matter what she saw, nor should she speak to him unless he addressed her first.

Chagrined by Erec's order, Enide set forth as briskly as she could. Thus, they had not traveled for more than half a day when they passed through a wood, and from afar, in a heath, she saw three thieves who were preparing to rob her, and they said to one another that her lovely jewels, palfrey, clothes, and mantle would not escape from them. Seeing the behavior of the thieves, Enide understood quite well that they intended to do wrong. She saw Erec, who pretended not to see them, and she did not dare to warn him for fear of troubling him, but nevertheless, Love conquers all, and there was no fear or dismay that kept her from turning towards her husband and saying to him, 'Oh, my lord, what are you thinking of doing? Save yourself

---

[14] 'Hurried off' inserted to fill a lacuna, following Foerster's suggestion, p. 269; also noted by Colombo Timelli, p. 215.

and me, or we will be robbed and put to death by three thieves who are lying in wait for us in this wood.'

'Ah, lady,' said Erec, 'didn't you hear my distinct command? How dare you speak to me when I have forbidden it? You take little heed of me and my words. In fact, I pardon you this time, but if ever it happens again, I know quite well what I have in mind to do.'

[p. 174] 20. *How Erec killed three brigands*

Thereupon Enide turned around and very fearfully set out on the path, for there appeared at once one of the brigands, armed and mounted, lance in hand, who sprang forward and called out to Erec that he was dead. Upon hearing this call, Erec challenged him, so the two spurred their good horses forward and came together impetuously. The thief failed to dismount Erec, and with all his strength Erec gave him such a blow of the lance on the shield that he broke it, split the hauberk, and pierced through to the brigand's heart so that he made him fall to the ground, dead. When the second robber saw his companion down, he galloped towards Erec, thinking to avenge his companion, but at their encounter, he broke his lance against Erec's shield. Erec seized him with all his strength and hurled him to the ground so roughly that he broke his leg and completely stunned him. Once this was done, Erec wanted to test the third man, but when the thief saw the bad bargain, the most heroic deed he did was to turn his back and flee as hastily as he could. Erec, who was well mounted, hurried after him, and when he could speak to him, he cried out, 'False churl with a cowardly heart! Turn around! Turn back and defend yourself, or I'll kill you in flight!'

Despite this exclamation, the thief had no desire to turn back; rather, he continued to spur forward, and Erec hastened after and caught up with him, then gave him such a blow between his collar and his headgear[15] that he knocked him down dead and delivered the world from him. Erec took the horse, and on his way back, found the other two that had belonged to his enemies. He rounded them up, and he killed the second thief whom he had knocked down through sheer force, then returned to Enide and had her set forth with the three horses, ordering her to be sure to refrain from speaking to him.

21. *How Erec killed five brigand knights, one after the other*

Thus Erec and Enide traveled until about six o'clock in the afternoon. They entered a large deserted region; at the foot of a mountain that they must descend, they see five fully armed knights, [p. 175] each with his shield hanging from

---

[15] 'Chapel', perhaps a simple iron cap or a 'chapel de fer', a kettle helmet.

around his neck and his lance in hand, for they have already seen Erec and Enide, the latter leading three horses. They are very joyful, thinking indeed that they have easily earned their day's work, and they predict that each of them will have a horse as his tip. The greatest master of these robber-knights says he will have the lady or die trying for her, and another one says he will be content to have the palfrey upon which she sits. The third says that for his booty he would like a black horse that belonged to the thieves. The fourth only wants a white courser, and the fifth does not fail to draw a good lot, for he swears that the knight's arms will be his as well as his charger. At this point, his companions let him have his say, for they fear the first blows.

Thereupon, this fifth brigand got completely ready and set out in front of the others. Erec definitely saw him, but he pretended not to, in order to test Enide, who did not know what to say. Therefore, she was deeply melancholy. She trembled like a leaf on a tree, and Love came before her to give advice, saying, 'My very beautiful friend, what are you thinking of doing when you see with your own eyes the trap that is being set for your lord and husband by these traitorous murderers who do not live on anything other than robbing and pillaging? Alas! Are you more subject to an edict than you are to warning him for his own good? Do you prefer to let him be taken by surprise and killed rather than informing him about the thieves who have sworn his death?'

'Certainly not,' said Enide. 'If he dies, I die. And because I cannot see him be hurt, I will turn back towards him, and even if he kills me at once, I will tell him what's on my heart.' Thereupon Enide turned back towards Erec, saying fearfully, 'Ah, lord, as dear as you hold your life, turn around and think about your situation, for down here in this valley, behind a clump of bushes, I have seen five brigands who are lying in wait for you, and if they can, they will injure you.'

'Oh, my wife,' said Erec, 'I would have thought that you would take more account of my words than you [p. 176] do. Now I see that you love my anger just as much as my joy. Upon my faith, it's badly done, and perhaps bad things will come of it for you.'

With these words Erec had to couch his lance, for the brigand came to attack him without a challenge. They charged each other without saying a word. Erec struck his enemy and threw him to the ground so hard that his heart gave out. Seeing this, one of the four brigands who had remained behind, on one side and the other, spurred his horse, and very angrily came to strike Erec so roughly that he broke his lance against his hauberk. Upon this attack, Erec struck his adversary on the side and lifted him out of the saddle, making him fall on his head, so that he broke his neck. Then out of another bush came the third brigand; he assaulted Erec on what was for him a bad day, for with a single blow Erec pierced his neck and knocked him down dead in great distress. Having seen this skirmish, the other two thieves marveled and said they would not wait around, for Erec seemed to be a devil rather than a mortal man. They fled, and Erec galloped after them. One of the horses stumbled and Erec, who continued to advance, hit the thief so roughly in passing that he made him fall against a dark stone so hard that his head was smashed and his arm broken, and he began to sigh because death was pursuing him. After having delivered himself from these four, Erec went for the fifth, who upon seeing that he could not escape, flung his arms afar – shield, helmet, hauberk, and sword – then dismounted and stood on the ground, crying out for mercy. Seeing his lack of courage, Erec did not deign to strike him; nevertheless, he took his horse and his lance and set out to return, rounding up all the other horses.

22. How Erec wanted Enide to lie down to sleep in the forest, but she refused, saying that he needed sleep more than she did

Enide was completely reassured when she saw Erec return, having overcome the five brigands. They set out on their way again, and in the evening [p. 177] around nightfall they entered a large forest. Erec wanted to sleep, so he stopped in a nook under a hawthorn surrounded with beautiful lush grass, then he told Enide to dismount from her palfrey. She did so, and when the horses were attached to a tree there, Erec told Enide that she should sleep and that he would watch.

'That I should sleep, my lord?' said Enide. 'Alas, it would be better if you did so, for you are more tired than I am.'

'Do as I say,' said Erec.

'No, I will not,' replied Enide, 'may it not displease you, for I prefer your repose to my own.'

This response made Erec very happy. He lay down on the grass, using his shield as a headrest, and as chance would have it, he was fairly comfortably installed. He fell asleep. Enide kept watch all night long, in deep thought, saying, 'Alas! Why was I ever born, when my dearly beloved lord must suffer this discomfort because of me, who sought this peril for him due to the false reports of his subjects? Oh, woe is me, I must certainly hate myself, for in him there is more prowess than in any other man, and his subjects were misled indeed when they said he forgot the noble exercise of the profession of arms.

'Oh, wise Solomon, you did not spread slander when you judged and declared that all of men's misfortunes, pestilences, and adversities come from women. You were very well informed about their deeds when you put in your book that women can hide nothing and that through their words great evils arise in the world. Certainly, I was born in an evil hour, since through me the words of the poets that say woman only harms man in every way are proved to be true, for it is not possible for woman to be perfected in keeping secrets like man is, he who would have known how to keep quiet if he had had to do as I did.'

With[16] deep regret Enide pronounced these words, and as long as night

---

[16] Colombo Timelli points out that this paragraph opens with a large red 'A', similar to the capital letters at the beginning of each chapter, following the rubric.

lasted, she kept on lamenting. When the sky was illumined by daylight, Erec, who was already awake, jumped to his feet, armed as he was, [p. 178] and prepared his gear. Then the two of them mounted their horses and set out on their route, leading the horses of the eight brigands. For a long time they traveled without finding any adventure that we must stop for. When they had come out of this great forest, at about ten o'clock, they perceived in the middle of the fields a squire and two servants who were carrying some flat breads, wine, and cheese to reapers who were working rather nearby in a field.

This squire also saw Erec and his beautiful lady, and he thought indeed that they had spent the night in a grove in the forest and needed to eat something. He went forward towards them and after exchanging greetings, the squire ventured to say to Erec, 'Sir knight, you who are wandering through this land, if you need bread or wine, don't hold back, for here is some in great plenty. From what I see, you are in great need of replenishing yourselves.'

'Friend,' said Erec, 'I thank you, and so that you don't believe I am refusing your offer, I will willingly partake of it, in exchange for equivalent satisfaction in deniers or something that is of equal worth.'

Thereupon Erec dismounted, as did his lady. The bread and wine were set out before them, and after they had eaten as much as they wanted, in remuneration for this pleasure, Erec gave the squire the choice of one of his horses. Thanking him, the squire went to look them over and took a very handsome black charger. He mounted it, and considered that his wine and bread had been put to good use.

Near this spot, about two leagues away, there was a large village and a castle. In order to allow his wife to rest, Erec went there to take lodgings at the home of a host who received them very joyfully and honored them deeply. But the squire, who could not contain himself because of his fine horse, went prancing through the streets. The lord of the castle saw him, and since this black seemed good to him, he enquired whose it was. 'It's mine,' said the squire.

This surprised the lord, so he asked where he had obtained it. The squire replied, 'Certainly, sir, a knight from a foreign land who has taken lodgings at a burgher's home gave it to me for a small service; but I tell you, never have you [p. 179] seen a man more well-built, nor wiser, more generous, polite, or charming.'

'Take care that you do not fail to tell the truth,' said the lord of the castle, 'for I know of no man more handsome than I in the world.'

'I don't wish to denigrate your beauty,' said the squire, 'but I assure you that this knight from a foreign land is of a very high rank and is a champion at armed combat: for the day before, he vanquished eight knights whose chargers he is leading as proof of this fact. Furthermore, his armor is in a terrible state. But so that you may know who is accompanying him, I assure you that he is with a lady who is the loveliest ever born and who would never be given to a knight if he weren't handsome beyond measure, like the one I have described to you.'

23. *How the lord of the castle beseeched Enide for her love*

When the lord of the castle heard these words, his entire heart opened up with joy because of the beautiful lady. It seemed to him indeed that if she saw his fine manly figure, she would love him. Thereupon he departed and went to the lodgings of Erec and Enide. He entered the room where they were refreshing themselves and, worn out, catching their breath. Upon entering, he greeted them, and they did not hesitate to respond. After conversing a little, this lord entreated Erec to join his retinue, offering him good wages. Erec, who would not deign to enter anyone's service for either gold or silver, responded that thank God, he did not need to serve anyone and that he was rich enough; so the lord did not go any further in his entreaty. He offered him lodging if it pleased Erec to accept his hospitality, but Erec refused everything.

'At least,' said the lord, 'may it please you that I converse with your lady to help her pass the time? For she seems to me to be plunged in thought.'

'Speak with her as much as you like,' said Erec. 'I don't wish to prevent you from that.'

'Thank you, sir,' said the lord, who then approached the beautiful woman, smiling at her covertly. He bowed before her as he approached. And she, who was well instructed in how to do honor, responded in kind, which [p. 180] made the lord fall more in love than before. He sat on the edge of a little bed and began to speak of love to her, saying, 'Oh my lady, why hasn't God given me the grace of attaining once in my life the love of such a noble lady as you are? Upon my faith, I would have her adored like a goddess, and you can be sure that never would anything she asked for be refused. Refused? Alas, he would indeed be ungracious, he who would contradict all the commands of such a beautiful lady, you who merit being loved by the highest prince in the world. Oh woe is me, why don't I have the power to ravish you invisibly! In truth, if such were the case, Love has so inflamed me with your beauty and polite manners, that you would immediately leave the company of this rude vassal, who is so presumptuous that he doesn't deign to speak or converse with you. For I who believe I am the most perfect of Nature's creations would be overjoyed if it pleased you to take me so well into your good graces that I could have the liberty to enjoy myself with you. And right now, my lady, I entreat you, behold my love, my beauty, and my power, over which you will be mistress, lady, and princess, if you wish to come with me.'

'Oh, sir knight,' replied Enide, 'keep your honor, and please do not attempt to vex any further the lady, unfortunate as she is, for she does not seek your vile and worthless offer.'

'What?' said the lord of the castle. 'Do you refuse the service of the most charming baron who reigns in the whole wide earth?'

'I have no need of your service,' said Enide, 'for I willingly accept the servant and master who has given himself to me, whose service I would reward badly if I were so out of my senses as to take a new lover, through my outrageous behavior. May God forbid it, and may it please God, I will never be reproached for such a great misdeed.'

[p. 181] 24. *How Enide advised Erec about the knight who wished to possess her through force*

God, how distressed this lord is when he cannot seduce or entice the good and beautiful lady according to his desire! He threatens to kill Erec at once if she does not give herself to him, and enraged Love enkindles him so much that it seems indeed he must perform wonders. Upon hearing this cursed churl – who is inflamed and excessively overheated – threaten Erec with death, Enide agrees to become his lover in order to save Erec's life. And since he is worn out and unarmed, she fixes a rendezvous for the next day. So this lord resolves that in the morning, he will come with a great number of men-at-arms and servants to kidnap Enide and kill Erec. And with these words, like a man who has lost his mind, he departs and, feigning friendship, takes leave of Erec. He goes to his castle, and Erec remains at his host's with Enide, to whom he does not speak.

Enide is very distracted, thinking about how she can escape from the control the lord has imposed on her. Night comes, and in a chamber with two beds, Erec and Enide lie down, each alone. Erec knows nothing about the affair between Enide and the lord. He sleeps confidently, something Enide does not do; rather, she is extremely weary, pensive, and wracked with nightmares. She hears the cock crow the third time, then when she sees daylight illuminating the world, she is afraid that the evil lord might come to take her friend in bed. Now she does not dare to awaken him because he has sworn to get angry with her if she speaks to him unless he has addressed her first. She gets up and looks intently out the window to see if she can see any sign of an assembly, and so much is her heart tortured by love, shame, and fear that she awakens her lover, Erec, and after saying good morning, she entreats him to be on his guard. She recounts how the lord of the city wanted to kill him the day before because she would not agree to love him and the fact that in order to save him, she arranged for the lord to come seek her this morning. 'Because', she said, [p. 182] 'I knew very well that if you rested during the night, you would have no need to fear him.'

25. *How Erec killed the lord of the castle as well as his seneschal*

Very distressed was Erec when he heard the wrong that the lord wished to commit against his most beloved lady. He had his horses bridled and saddled; then he called his host, and once he had paid him, he departed, armed and well mounted, and set forth in order to be in open country. Now may God, who has the power, guide Erec and Enide safely. The two lovers have left, and as he did earlier, Erec forbade Enide to speak to him.

Meanwhile the lord of the city, having already made his preparations, secretly looked out a window and saw in the fields the knight and lady galloping rapidly away. Then he realized that he had been deceived, so he cried out, 'Now, quickly, handsome knights, on your horses, for the knight from the foreign land is taking his lover away with him and has already left his lodgings. After him! After him! By my faith, the one who can present me with his head will receive such a gift that he will be very pleased!'

Then knights and men-at-arms mount their horses. They head for the fields, galloping as fast as they can, as quickly as the horses can go. They have left the city far behind before they manage to see Enide, who is departing at a fast pace. Finally, they pursue her so much that they perceive the couple before their very eyes quite near a forest; they are so joyful that they give full rein to their horses in order to catch up with them more quickly. They make so much noise that Enide, hearing it, cannot keep from looking back. She sees the lord and his large company descending through a valley, and one need not ask if she is frightened at seeing such a great number of men. She is overwhelmed; indeed, she is so lost that she does not remember her friend's order, so she says to him, 'My friend, God, [p. 183] my lord, what shall we do? Look at these enemies! In truth, if they can, they will hurt you, and me as well. I beg of you, let us hasten! It seems to me that, God willing, if we can once get into the forest, we can turn so far off their path that they won't be able to find us and their malevolence will be deflected.'

Enide had barely finished her remarks when the lord's seneschal, galloping and striking out, neared Erec, who turned around and immediately went to hit him in such a way that he pierced him completely through and knocked him to the ground dead. Thereupon came the lord of the castle, who was so overconfident in his strength that he had not deigned to take any other arms than his lance and shield. He saw Erec, who had killed his seneschal, which did not make him very happy; in order to avenge his death, he spurred forward against Erec and struck his shield so roughly that he pierced it and shattered his lance against the hauberk. And if Erec had not been firmly in his stirrups, the lord would easily have brought him to the ground.

After this blow, the story says that Erec rewarded him in such a way that he pierced completely through his shield and body and, bringing sudden death, knocked him off his charger, which fled, galloping off across the plains. This done, Erec went off into the forest, at a good pace. And soon, there arrived his enemies, who found their lord and the seneschal dead on the spot. They did not dare pursue Erec; rather, defeated, crying, and cursing the day, they set out to return to the city, taking with them the two dead men in great grief and sadness.

26. *How Guivret le Petit pursued Erec and how Enide lamented*
when she saw him coming

As you have heard, Erec delivered himself from his enemies, and when he
had traveled for a long time, both through the forest and through several
deserted areas, he found himself before a bridge seated over a big river that
lapped against the wall of a great tower. He and Enide crossed this bridge,
then they continued on, but they had only gone a short [p. 184] distance
when the lord of this tower, whose name was Guivret le Petit, saw them
pass by. He said he would go after them and had himself lightly armed in
a hauberk, helmet, and greaves. Then he mounted his good charger, and
once he had his shield hanging around his neck, his lance in hand, and his
sword at his side, he left his house and, in order to head off Erec, he set off
all alone, taking the shortcuts.

This lord did so well that he sighted Erec and his lady-love in a valley,
and then his horse began to neigh and paw the ground and kick so violently
that it made sparks fly from the dark stones. The lady heard this noise and
was suddenly so overcome that she nearly fell in a faint from her palfrey.
Her blood curdled, and there was not a single vein that was not affected by
this sudden fright. She became as inflamed as fire, then in a minute as pale
as death, and she was so distraught that she knew not what to do or say.

She wanted to speak to her lover and lord, but, alas, she did not dare to,
so her anguish was renewed: for, given that she did it for his good, she was
deeply frustrated by the fact that she must be deprived of the much-desired
discussion that a lord and lady should have with each other. Regarding
this debatable matter she talked to herself and often turned her tongue so
as to speak, but her voice did not dare come out, because he would become angry with her. Then she clamped her mouth shut so that she did not
say something that would displease her dear one, but unexpectedly, Love
abruptly struck her heart so that she perspired, and it seemed she must die
from deep distress. So she said, 'Oh, woe is me, what a sad day when I see
my lord's mortal enemy approaching to assail him, and yet he isn't on his
guard! Alas! How can it be that he doesn't see him! How could I be so
false as to not forewarn him of this danger? Upon my soul, I would be too
cowardly if I didn't tell him to watch out. Therefore, even if he were to kill
me on the spot, I'll warn him. For I know that after my death God would
have pity and compassion on my soul, and I would calm God's wrath if he
wished to take vengeance, for despite any ill that my husband might do to
me, I could never hate him. Because [p. 185] of this, people say, and I don't
doubt it: he who loves well is slow to forget. And as for me, my love is so
well secured and enclosed that, even if he did all the evils in the world to
me, I would bear them willingly for love of him.'

With these words, Enide turned back towards her lord and, with copious
tears streaming from her eyes, she ventured to say to him, 'Oh, my friend,
turn around and look who's following you! Noble knight, save your life!'

For these words Erec scolded Enide, but he had no desire to harm her, for he knew through experience that she loved him with such a love that none deeper could exist, for this love fears neither forbiddance nor any other thing; rather it is so ardent that it conquers all.

27. How Erec and Guivret jousted together, and afterwards fought with their swords

Erec heard and felt his enemy approach, so he turned around, and Guivret incited him to defend himself. Erec saw his adversary was eager to join in combat, so he challenged him, and thereupon, the good knights spurred towards one another. They couched their lances when the time came, and they ran together with such force that their sturdy shields and mesh hauberks were not powerful enough to withstand the iron tips of their lances. They wounded each other, drawing abundant blood, but no wound was mortal. And due to the difficulty the good chargers had in sustaining these blows, they stopped in their tracks, for they could not move forward until the knights had pulled their lances out of each other's bodies. Because the lances were not broken, the two men drew back from one another, then with all their might they hit each other's shields so violently that they shattered their lances, and pieces of them flew up as high as six lance-lengths.

Then they came together again, [p. 186] running against each other so precipitously that both of them fell to the ground. After this high venture and vigorous joust, they drew their good swords, and in great furor began this combat with the greatest blows they could give, with all their strength. God knows the shields were well tested! The two men use them to cover themselves, receiving on them the heavy blows of the swords. And the most beautiful sport they play together is to rip apart hauberks, helmets, and shields with the sharp edges of their steel blades, which they blunt by striking over and over with all their might. Both of them are passionate in this continuous labor, and from the hour of tierce to nones they do not cease going after one another, for neither one of them is lacking a heart governed by a strong will, so much so that they would rather lose most of their blood than to give up.

28. How Erec broke Guivret's sword, causing the latter to grieve deeply

The very loyal lady Enide watches the combat between the two knights, who test each other very roughly; she is unable to control her emotions, and often she nearly falls from her palfrey in a faint. It is not necessary to ask whether she expresses regrets, sighs, tears, and exclamations. No one could do more than she, and she even torments herself with such great distress that, if God does not bring her friend happily out of this combat, she will be so deeply saddened that in order to compensate for such a loss, she will let herself die. Harder and harder do the two stout-hearted knights fight one another. They strike wondrous blows, and no one can say who has the best of it, for they have wounded each other, and the blood flows from their wounds, so that it is a pity to see two such noble men hurt each other without cause or reason. Rightly or wrongly, hour after hour they are still hard at work. Among his blows to his enemy, Erec deals one downwards onto the helmet [p. 187] so that he breaks it and goes in to the quick.

Pride wells up in the knight who feels himself wounded in this way, and despite this cruel blow, he raises his sword and strikes, believing he will smite Erec on his helmet, but Erec is on his guard. He thrusts his shield out in front, and the sword, which is very slender, goes in and at the shock breaks half a foot from the hilt. Now Guivret is in a pitiful state of confusion; Erec is very joyful, for he does not doubt that the honor of this enterprise will be his. Thereupon he recovers his senses, and presses more strongly his adversary, who becomes frightened, and like someone who does not know what cards to play, disdainfully throws the remnant of his sword far away, and says, 'Noble knight, what more do you want from me, I who am deprived of arms? Certainly, if you kill me, the honor will be small, given that I have neither battle-ax nor sword; and if you did that, your prestige would be lessened.'

'These treacherous words will not convince me,' said Erec, 'for may God never help me again, if I don't vanquish you. And if you do not put yourself at my mercy, I'll do with your body what seems best to me.' Erec ceased his work for a while, believing that the knight would give himself up to him courteously, but this was not yet the case. He did not say a word in reply to Erec's speech, like someone who is very distraught at having to give up, seeing that he had sought out this misfortune. When Erec saw the way things were, he raised up his sword and brandished it, and when he pretended to approach Guivret, this Guivret was so frightened that in the best way he knew, he compelled his heart to be humble and cried out, 'Mercy, sir knight, mercy! To you I give up willingly, entreating you to take pity on me and to pardon the venture that I undertook with you in order to maintain chivalry's noble custom.'

Seeing the knight kneel before him begging for mercy, Erec told him that he need no longer have fear, since he considered himself vanquished, and asked his name. 'Guivret I am called, sir lord, and I am the lord of this land, which because of the courteous manners I've found in you is at your command. And I entreat you to come rest in my lodgings until you and I are healed of our wounds. And afterwards, if you wish to go somewhere, [p. 188] I will be completely at your disposition, to accompany you and be your brother-at-arms.'

Erec thanked him, stating that he had undertaken a journey such that he would never turn back from his route until he had accomplished his objective. But Erec entreated him very strongly that if he ever heard he needed his help, he should come to his assistance. Guivret promised to do so every time he was needed, if he learned of it; and after taking leave as good friends, which came after their mortal and cruel battle, they separated.

Erec headed back on his way and had Enide set forth on the route, and they did not stop until arriving in the evening at a hermit's little hut, where they rested for the night. The next day they set forth, traveling until they reached an area of open country; very nearby they saw a large forest in which King Arthur, the queen, and the barons had come to divert themselves at that point in time. And by chance, Kay, the seneschal, upon seeing Erec approach, went to the lodges and found Sir Gauvain's armor, horse, sword, and lance near a tree. He had himself fitted out in all this gear by a squire of his, and once he was mounted on the Gringalet, he set out to head off Erec and came to meet him, taking him by the horse's bit without greeting the couple. Erec was not very happy about this, and despite being wounded, he said to him, 'Vassal, let me continue on my way, for you have been urged on by an overly cowardly heart in taking my horse's bit without saying a word. I thought I knew you and would have said many good things about you, but I would have been lying.'

Upon hearing Erec speak, Kay asked who he was, where he was coming from, and what he intended to do with the beautiful lady, whom he did not recognize because she had pulled her wimple over her face to protect it from the heat and the dust. When Erec heard Kay answer so rudely, wanting to know his name, he replied that first he would have to win from him the right to know this, and that otherwise he would not learn it. 'And right now', said Erec, 'if you wish to demand anything of me, I challenge you.'

[p. 189] 29. *How Erec jousted with Kay the seneschal and unhorsed him on the first blow*

At these words Kay distanced himself from Erec; he couched his lance, and the two good knights spurred their chargers and met in a joust with such force that Erec made Kay's shield strike his helmet so hard that it stunned him and sent him to the ground, dazed. Erec seized the Gringalet and gave it to Enide to hold, and Kay, who was embarrassed, got up and surrendered to Erec, imploring him to return the Gringalet, since it belonged to Sir Gauvain.

'For Sir Gauvain's honor, in whose name you claim it,' replied Erec, 'I'm very pleased to return it to you,' which filled Kay with joy. He thanked Erec, then mounted the horse, and after taking leave, galloped off to King Arthur to recount his adventure with the knight who had unhorsed him at the first course of the lance. 'But,' said Kay the knight, 'I'm telling you that the knight is worn out, for he hasn't a single piece of armor that isn't cut to pieces or ripped apart, and it seems that for the past two weeks he hasn't done anything other than fight, using one hauberk, one helmet, and one shield. In fact, I looked carefully to see if I could recognize his arms, but upon my soul, they are so damaged that there is no appearance at all of paint – only of blood – with which they are completely covered.'

Upon hearing this news, the king did not know what to think. He sent Sir Gauvain after Erec, telling him that if he could do so in any way, he should bring the knight to him and offer him gold, silver, service, money, and himself, if he needed him. Sir Gauvain said he would willingly do so. He mounted a horse and along with two squires, pursued Erec until he caught up with him. He greeted him nobly. Erec returned his greeting, and then Sir Gauvain proceeded to say to him, 'Sir knight, I implore you on the part of King Arthur, in whom all honor and wisdom abound, that it please you to come join him in this wood and partake of his goods. He has heard that you are badly wounded, so he has taken pity on you, and [p. 190] because of the good things that his seneschal has told him about you, may it please you to not refrain from taking gold, silver, guides to accompany you, or any other thing. Before you go any further, I beg of you, please come to him, and he will honor you greatly.'

'Many thanks to him,' said Erec, 'and to you, my noble lord, but pardon me, for I'm not at my ease. Furthermore, there is something that keeps me from going there: I would go against my oath if I turned back before completing the venture I have undertaken.'

30. *How Sir Gauvain recognized Erec and Enide and welcomed them joyfully*

When Sir Gauvain realized that there was no way that he could get Erec to turn back, he sent one of his squires to the king, with a message that if he wished to see the knight, he must hastily have his pavilions loaded up and go set them up the shortest way along this route by which the knight must pass. Upon hearing this message, the king promptly did what Sir Gauvain had recommended, and in great haste, the tents were quickly set up again.

So Erec, seeing Sir Gauvain leading him along slowly and questioning him about various things, entreated him to let him pursue his route all alone, stating that he was detaining him a good deal. In order to prolong things, Sir Gauvain used several delaying tactics, saying that one could not always move along at a horse-killing pace. As he said these words, Erec saw King Arthur's pavilions, marked with his coat of arms. He saw very well that he could no longer hide his identity, so he said, 'Alas! Now I see very well that despite all my efforts, my name and that of my lady must be disclosed. So, Sir Gauvain, I wish to inform you that I am Erec, and here is my wife, whom I am taking with me alone on a trip to accomplish a vow I made, which [p. 191] will not be revealed to anyone.'

When Sir Gauvain heard these words, he quivered with joy; he unlaced Erec's helmet and embraced him gently, with the greatest delight in the world. Then he went to welcome the beautiful lady, asking her if there was anything she needed and how she fared.

'Alas, my lord,' said Enide, 'my health would be quite good if it weren't for my lord's wounds. Certainly, there isn't a drop of blood that has been shed that I have not dearly bought.'

Sir Gauvain marveled at this reply, for he found her as prudent as he had ever found any lady. He kissed her out of great love. And to be brief, as joyful as anyone can be, he went to recount to the king that Erec was the knight he had been told about. Very gladdened was the king. He told the queen, who was filled with new delight, as were his barons. They came out of the tents and pavilions to go join the much-loved knight, Erec. Upon seeing him, the king and queen went to meet him with open arms. Erec and Enide dismounted, then before them came the king, who did what is customary in order to welcome his friend. The king embraced and kissed Enide, while Erec, for his part, embraced and kissed the queen, and God knows what joyous demonstrations of friendship were performed at this welcoming.

After welcoming Erec and Enide, the king led them to his pavilion. Erec was disarmed, and as someone needing care, his wounds were bandaged and treated with a precious and potent ointment that the king gave him. About the supper and pastimes that took place that evening our account will be silent. The site was full of delight, but as soon as night fell, Erec took leave of the king and the queen, who were very saddened by his quick departure. Erec was put to bed gently in a bed all alone; Enide slept in the same bed as the queen, who cherished her and loved her deeply. That night Enide slept very well, like someone who had not had a single hour of rest for the previous three days. And when the next day came, once gracious good-byes were said to the queen, Enide – finding that Erec was already dressed, mounted, and armed – got on her palfrey, and thus they left. They rode until tierce without finding any adventure worth recounting.

They entered a wood, and once they had been on the high road for a while, Erec heard a young woman's voice; she was crying piteously, 'Alas! Alas!' Erec, who [p. 192] willingly served ladies, left his beloved there, telling her he would go see what was happening. He spurred his good horse to the gallop and found the sad and tearful girl. He greeted her and enquired about her grievance: 'My beautiful girl, take some comfort and speak to me bravely; tell me your misfortune, and if there is some pleasing thing I might do for you in order to lighten your suffering, I am ready to set to it.'

The maiden lifted her troubled face, covered with copious tears, then in an unhappy voice, speaking sadly, ventured to say, 'Oh, noble knight who stops on his way at the side of a disconsolate damsel and asks about her hard misfortune, may you know that the cause is not small, for two false and outrageous giants have taken my very dear lover from me and, despite my outcry, are leading him away completely nude, hitting and striking him roughly, which is why I ask only for death, in order to be killed more quickly than he who is being taken away – he who will die a terrible death today if God does not rescue him.'

'My lovely maiden,' said Erec, 'pluck up your spirits, and do not yet plunge into such great despair, for I promise you that I will die on the spot or bring back your friend without any delay as one who, in consideration of Love and compassion for your grief, will be your champion today.'

'May God grant that you return in joy,' said the maiden. 'Take this road. Until you return I shall be in prayer, begging God to help you. No matter what adventure might befall me, I will not move from this spot until I have received a reliable report regarding your exploit.'

31. How Erec killed two giants, one after the other, in a wood

Erec hurried off, following the tracks of the two giants, and he had not gone very far on his way when he saw the maiden's friend on a horse, tied up [p. 193] very tightly and tortured more roughly than can be stated. Now, these two giants had no other weapons than two heavy, weighty clubs. Erec caught up with them, and as soon as he could, he proceeded to say, 'My lords, you who are taking this prisoner away, give him to me in a friendly way, at my request, for the sake of the love and rightful claim of his lady, whose servant I am, and you will do a good and noble deed.'

'Vassal,' replied one of the giants, 'you're undertaking a deeply foolish thing, for we will not return the knight to you; instead, we will torture him in this grove without stopping until we have killed him.'

Erec said, 'On your guard, then! Because of the complaint, request, and supplication of his loyal lady, who is deeply grieved, I will put myself in danger, come what may.' Then he spurred his horse forward, and came to the first giant in such a way that he struck him in the eye with the sharp iron lance-head, driving it into the brain until this first blow made him fall down dead. Once this was done, the second giant, who saw that Erec's lance was broken, came forward to attack him; he raised his square club, thinking he would hit him on the head and strike him down, but Erec put his shield out in front and received the blow on it. He then drew his sword and brought it down from high above onto the top of the giant's head so roughly that he split it open down to the teeth, and made the giant fall down dead with the other one. Thus Erec came to the end of his enterprise, for which he praised God.

32. How Erec pretended to be dead when he returned to Enide

After these deeds, Erec went to the knight, who could not thank him enough. He untied him and had him get dressed; then the two returned to the spot where the maiden was. Upon seeing her beloved, her sorrow quickly turned to happiness; she thanked Erec a hundred thousand times, and the knight he had delivered did more, presenting him with his service. Erec [p. 194] asked him what his name was and who he was, to which the knight replied, 'I am yours and hold myself to be yours. My name is Cadoc, whom you can order to do what you like in return for the unrewarded good, high deed that you have done for me by your grace.'

'As for that,' replied Erec, 'thank God! Since you've been delivered from the hands of your enemies, if you please, you and your lady friend will go to King Arthur, and since you deign to do a service for me in recompense, you will recount your situation and present your service on my behalf.'

The knight and maiden promised to do what Erec asked and later acquitted themselves of it very well. They set out on their way and traveled until they reached the court of King Arthur and the queen. After exchanging greetings, they presented themselves at the king and queen's service, and once they had recounted Erec's deeds, they were retained as part of the household, and for love of Erec, they were deeply honored.

At this point we will return to speak about Erec, who after this deliverance, returned as quickly as he could to the spot where he had left Enide. But, as the story says, when he was about to draw near to her, either his wounds reopened and began to bleed because of the heat and the exertion he had undergone, or in order to test the loyal heart of his lady, he got off his horse and fell beside a small tree that was rather near his wife. It could appear to her that he was quite unwell, which caused her to break into a sweat out of distress, because Erec feigned to be dead or in great danger.

33. How Enide lamented over the death of Erec, whom she saw suddenly fall

Enide, the very trustworthy, beautiful lady, upon seeing that Erec had fallen without a word, ran to him in complete despair and began to speak softly to him while unlacing his helmet. But, wishing to test her, he closes his eyes and holds his breath, and despite anything that Enide does or says, he gives no sign [p. 195] of being alive. Because of this, such a ray of despair comes to trouble her emotions that her heart fails her, and she falls down in a dead faint. Then, when she regains consciousness, she kisses and embraces her beloved, weeping piteously. Once she has embraced and kissed him a hundred times without his showing any sign of life, she – the unhappiest woman in the world – rips her clothes off and, as if undone, scratches her face, then grabs her hair and tears it out with both hands, in the deepest unhappiness that woman has ever endured. She falls over again, as if half-dead. Now she no longer controls her emotions and no longer has the strength to address her beloved. Over and over she faints while getting up; then, looking at Erec lying stretched out, from her full height she falls to the ground. Never has anyone seen greater anguish expressed. Before she is able to speak, she is full of sorrow – so much so that no one could possibly tell of it.

After these fainting spells, her whole body overcome with fatigue, she recovered the power of speech and began a complaint in this way: 'Oh, most unfortunate lady, who has been knocked down from on high to the very lowest by one of Fortune's trebuchets, what will you do, poor woman – you, who are a murderer and the cause of the death[17] of the very loyal knight, my lord Erec, who was a short time ago inspired by the grace of Love? Oh, what harsh words when I spoke to him about the exercise of arms! Upon my soul, I should certainly hate myself, since I am guilty of the death of my own husband in whose body beauty itself was mirrored, wisdom diffused, honor planted, prowess lodged. Chivalry, goodness, generosity, and integrity had fashioned him as the most perfect person who will ever exist! Oh what a wretched woman I can consider myself to be! Woe is me, what will become of me after this great loss that the world undergoes in the person of this noble knight? What kind of death will be meted out to me? And what penance will be given to me to compensate for this terrible crime that occurred because of me? Alas, if only I had known the cursed outcome of this affair when I revealed my thoughts to him! Upon my soul, I would rather have torn out my tongue with both hands than let it utter the unfortunate words! Ah, what will this poor woman become? Because of her trouble and [p. 196] very sorry misfortune, I must die. I want death, and I would like to be dead already, if only my lord could still be alive.'

We must therefore not ask how many regrets, what grievous sighs and sobs, nor what tears Enide poured forth while pronouncing these words; but in order to praise more fully the love of this loyal lady, we can say that along comes Despair, rushing towards her, invisibly enlacing her in his nets and admonishing her ardently in this way: 'Oh, you, you must be the lady in the world who most desires the end of your days and the brief hour of your life after the death of your lord, who through your exhortations, has fallen into this danger. May you care no longer to live, for if you remain in the world, you will stay as a lost soul, lacking in goodness and honor, as the most wretched woman ever born. Never will your tears come to an end; instead, you shall languish and torment yourself with more anguish than any other woman, no matter how wretched. Therefore, in order to take vengeance for the death that you have caused, I know of nothing more reasonable than that you should die. And thus, if you die, there will be no reason to file a complaint against you, since for love of him, to satisfy this loss, you will have killed yourself. In order that you may have a good witness, take his sword and point it towards your heart; then let yourself fall on it as Thisbe did for love of her beloved Piramus, and you will obtain great praise in this world and reward for your body.'

At that the lady is completely out of her senses, separated from hope, her head emptied of its senses, her heart ensnared in distress; sad and full of imagined things. In order to sacrifice herself, she advances, and like a woman who has lost her mind, she takes her husband's sword, and with Despair's permission, is already pointing it towards her heart, calling out to Death, 'Take this wretch!' when the count of Limors, who was passing nearby, hearing this cry, understands very well by the feebleness of her voice

---

[17] 'Death' inserted, as per the editor's suggestion, p. 216, to fill a lacuna.

that she is in despair. So he hurries there with his noble entourage, and God knows how distressed he is upon seeing that this beautiful lady is holding the sword with which she wishes to kill herself. As quickly as he can, the count dismounts, and greatly troubled, embraces the grieving lady, [p. 197] takes the sword from her hands and puts it back in Erec's scabbard. And Enide, who does not have leisure to obey Despair's admonition, falls in a faint, and it seems that she will never be joyful again. The count raises her up and after his gracious greeting, asks her if the dead knight is her lord husband or beloved.

'He is both to me,' she affirmed. 'Thus, so help me God, I would like to be one hundred feet under ground, so that I can never escape death.'

'Oh, what sad and piteous words!' said the count. 'My lovely friend, think about taking comfort, for your grieving could be the cause of too great a loss for God and Nature. I shall take you to be my wife, and I will make you a princess over my land; and for love of you, I will bury your husband solemnly.'

'Ah, lord, for God's sake, let this poor wretch die in obscurity, for I will never have anything to do with joy, comfort, life, or happiness; instead, I am determined to die rather than leave here.'

With these words Enide fell in a deep faint. And the count had a bier made, stating that he would inter the knight at Limors, and that he would marry the lady, whether she wished it or not. The bier was prepared, and Erec, once his helmet was laced up again, was laid on it; and it was tied to two horses so that he could not fall. Then the count, ravished by love because of the lady's beauty, raised her up forcibly and set her behind him on the horse, carrying her away, as sad as she was. He and his men set off on their way, traveling slowly until they reached Limors.

34. *How Erec killed the count of Limors*

When the count saw that he had arrived, he had a tomb built hastily in order to inter Erec, whom he placed in a hall. Enide was there weeping piteously, and the count sent for ladies and damsels to comfort this disconsolate lady, but nothing they said could diminish her tears. In the end the chaplain came, who married Enide to the count, whether she wished or not. The tables were set up, and when dinnertime came, [p. 198] the count took the tear-stained Enide by the hand, wishing to have her sit down at the table, willingly or not, despite her repeated refusals. And thereupon, here is Erec, who no longer wishes to feign death, or who regains consciousness from his faint, and has heard the situation of his lady. Suddenly he jumps up and draws his good sword that was still girded, comes to strike the count on the top of his head and knocks him down dead in the presence of all his men, who have never been so frightened. They believe Erec is a devil and flee, each as best he can, trembling and horribly scared. As they go out the door, Erec kills a great number of them. Finally, he comes to Enide, very joyfully, and calms her a little. He then leaves the premises and, en route, meeting a boy who is returning from taking his own horse to drink, goes to him and grabs the reins out of his hands, knocks him down, then mounts and sets Enide behind him. They head off, and in a short time they cross out of the city and take to the fields.

But now we will leave off speaking of Erec for a little and will come around to recount that Guivret had heard by chance that a dead knight had been found in a wood with a very beautiful, sad lady next to him, crying over the knight's death; and that despite her protests, the count of Limors had taken her away, as well as the body of the dead knight. This news made Guivret very anxious; remembering Erec and his lady, he said that he would go to rescue her from the lord of Limors and that he would bring back with him the body of the dead knight and have it buried with great dignity. He assembled a thousand men-at-arms, and on the very day that Enide had been led away, he set forth in great haste.

Both parties entered the wood at about the same time and took such a route that they met up with each other. Erec heard the noise of a cavalcade and, surprised, did not know what to do. He spoke to his lady about the situation and had her dismount near a thicket, where she was to hide until the army passed by. The lady did so willingly; and immediately along came Guivret, who was riding out in front of the others. The moon was shining. Guivret perceived Erec from afar, and because he saw him wearing [p. 199] armor, with shield, hauberk, and helmet, he cried out to him to prepare himself to joust for love of the ladies, for that was how he wished to welcome him.

35. How Guivret knocked Erec down in one course with the lance, which saddened him very much afterwards

When Erec heard Guivret – despite the fact that he was tired from bearing arms and that he was so weak from the blood he had lost and from not having eaten that he could barely stay in his saddle – nevertheless, with the great strength of heart with which he was endowed, not wanting to fail for just one joust, so that he would not be blamed for cowardice, he put his hand to his sword, since he did not have a lance. And with whatever effort he could muster, he spurred towards Guivret, who met him so roughly that he brought Erec to the ground, for he was barely worth more than a dead man. Guivret advanced so as to have him swear to be his prisoner; but Enide, who saw her beloved fallen to the ground, sprang forward and at once went to Guivret to beg for mercy. 'For', said she, 'you can see that he is very badly wounded and that he is unable to get up.'

Guivret took pity on her and swore to her that he would not seek anything further. 'But,' said he, 'my beautiful lady, you will please tell me his name; when I know what it is, for love of you, I will have him accompanied safely.' Hearing Guivret's assurance, Enide replied that his name was Erec, the most loyal knight alive. As soon as Guivret heard her speak of Erec, he immediately dismounted and kneeled before Erec, telling him how he was on his way to Limors to rescue him, and that it had been affirmed that he was dead. 'And so that you may know my name and recognize me, I am Guivret, and if I have wronged you in any way, I beg your pardon.'

God knows that Erec was soothed in his suffering and filled with joy. The two men embraced each other. Erec recounted his adventure, and after sweet demonstrations of friendship, Guivret took Erec that night to rest in a castle of his [p. 200] that was fairly near by, where Guivret's two beautiful and noble sisters were. They treated Erec with good ointments and bandaged him up so well with Enide's good help that they healed him before two weeks had passed. Erec was administered to with baths, hot tubs, and other comforts, and after his wounds had been healed, acknowledging Enide's love for him, he kissed and embraced her and went to bed with her as he had been accustomed to do. And you must know that their joy was not small at the moment of this renewed acquaintance; and everything Erec had done was only to test Enide, whom he found to be as loyal, and more, towards her husband than any other woman, so that ever since then he was more in love with her than he had been before.

36. How Erec arrived in the city of Brandigan and inquired about the site and to whom the place belonged

What more shall I tell you? Seeing that he was at liberty and healed of his wounds, Erec called Guivret and told him that he wanted to go to King Arthur's court. Guivret replied that he would accompany him, so he prepared his gear and gave Erec as a present a splendid outfit made of cloth of gold; to Enide, he gave another present: a very handsome palfrey with equipment entirely studded with emeralds, pearls, and gold buttons. The saddle was of an unusual design: it was covered with pourpre and had saddle-bows made of ivory; they were gilded and carved so artfully that the story of Dido and Aeneas was there enchased; and the story states that it had taken the artisan five years to make it. The final outcome was that Enide did not refuse the present, and after gracious adieux and humble thanks to the young ladies who were Guivret's sisters, knights, ladies, and squires mounted their horses and traveled so far, heading [p. 201] towards King Arthur's court, that they found themselves one evening at the castle at Brandigan, indeed inside the city.

Erec asked Guivret what this region was called, and Guivret stated the name, adding that it belonged to King Evrain, who had his residence there. 'But,' said he, 'the castle is such a stronghold that if all the men who are and who will be in the world besieged it, they could not take it, for inside there is an orchard that never fails to have fresh fruit and flowers, be it winter or summer. Nor is there a man bold enough to penetrate inside it or carry arms because of an adventure that is there.'

37. *How King Evrain came out to meet Erec*

When Erec heard about the nature of the orchard and that there was an adventure, he adjured Guivret in God's name to tell him the truth about it. Guivret replied that he did not dare tell him because it concerned a chivalric feat; but he did not know what to do nor how to excuse himself enough, so he ended up having to say that many noble and valorous men had lost their lives in the orchard because they had tried to conquer through armed combat the Joy of the Court. 'However,' said Guivret, 'I can tell you no more.'

'Let us go spend the night there,' said Erec, who at that moment decided to risk his person and his life in order to find out what the Joy of the Court was. They entered the city and asked for lodging; but there was none, for King Evrain had forbidden everyone to provide lodgings to people connected to knighthood because he wanted to welcome and provide fine food to nobles passing through his kingdom. Burghers, ladies, and girls gazed at the handsome company, and among all of them, they looked at Erec because of his beauty, saying indeed to themselves and to each other that it would be too bad if such a handsome knight were to go to that spot to conquer [p. 202] the Joy of the Court.

Evrain heard about the arrival of the knights, so he went out to meet them and entreated them to spend the night in his lodgings. After being welcomed, Erec, the lady, and the barons dismounted and were led up inside the castle, into a luxuriously decorated hall. Suppertime came; tables were set up; knights and ladies stayed at table for a long time. After conversing about various things, Erec began speaking with Evrain; he told him he would fight the next day in order to acquire, if he could, the Joy of the Court. Evrain was deeply saddened when he heard Erec's plan, and he advised him quite strongly against undertaking the adventure in which such a great number of knights had lost their lives. Erec praised Evrain for the good advice he gave, and said that he was indeed a loyal lord. 'But, sir,' said Erec, 'God forbid that I should give up in a fight without striking a blow.' To these words Evrain did not respond.

About the conversations and entertainments of that night our tale will be silent. And to come to the point about the facts regarding the orchard, the next morning, Erec arose. He asked for his arms, and Evrain sent him very good ones: a sound shield, a strong lance, a massive helmet, and a hauberk equipped with tightly woven links. Erec put them on, helped by Enide and Guivret, but before he was fitted out, King Evrain came to say good morning. When Erec considered that he was well equipped in arms, he mounted a good charger. He was escorted by the king and his barons, indeed by most of the inhabitants of the city, to the orchard, which was made by magic in such a way that it was enclosed and surrounded by air alone and so could only be entered through a narrow passage.

Erec entered this pleasant spot, beautifully embellished with flowers, trees, and the like. Once he had advanced a short way, he found a tree loaded with knights' heads where a horn was hung. Erec asked the king where these heads came from; the king told him that if the battle did not bring honor to him, his head would have to be placed there; and if he were to have the upper hand, he would sound the horn; upon the horn-call the Joy of the Court would be given to him. 'And I will not advance any further,' said Evrain. 'Go forward along this way, and be [p. 203] on your guard. May God grant you good fortune.'

Evrain left, and Enide, who was very melancholy, fell at the feet of her lord, who dismounted to attend to her. And God knows the piteous tears that were suddenly sent there from the fountains of their hearts, through Love's will. Erec comforted his lady, embracing and kissing her; then after piteous adieux, he recommended her to the king of the heavens, as she did him. He mounted his charger again, and had hardly gone very far when he found in the shade of a sycamore a silver bed that was nobly decorated with all kinds of fine things. On it was a young woman who was blessed with very great beauty; Erec was about to go question her when, raising his head, suddenly he saw surge forward an armed knight on horseback, with his shield hung from around his neck and his lance in hand.

The knight cried out, 'Vassal, move back from the most beautiful woman in the world, for you aren't worthy of approaching her! Flee from this spot, or I will deprive you of your life and make you aware of the great offense that you are committing towards her, for I am the man who is the champion and servant of the lady, in whose service I remain, guarding the orchard and the Joy of the Court.'

38. *How Erec and the knight jousted together*

'Knight,' said Erec, 'when it pleases you, you will speak a little more courteously. Even though you are a foot taller than I, I am not at all afraid of your threats. You will speak[18] and I will let you do it, but you will just as well have spoken foolishly as very sensibly. And regarding your having cried out that I should flee, despite your showy posture, if it is to be that I am to win the Joy of the Court with the iron lance head and the blade of the sword, finally, the body is quite ready to risk its life and to await God's good grace and Fortune's destiny.'

At these words the young woman's champion defied Erec, who pulled back a little in order to execute his attack, then spurred towards his enemy. And the two approached each other so [p. 204] roughly that they pierced one another's shields, and had it not been for the strength of the hauberks and the weakness of the lances, which broke, they would have wounded each other grievously. Nevertheless, they took up new lances, which they

---

[18] The repetition of 'you will speak' could be a scribal error; see editor's note, p. 216.

broke. And on the third course,[19] since they had broken and shattered their lances, they came together so harshly that they both fell, as did their horses. Thereupon they must put their hands to their swords; once they have done so, they strike each other with the point and the cutting edge of the swords until their helmets send out sparks, and they make a great din, clashing on each other's shields. They are ardent in this noble occupation, so they do not cease delivering blows, nor advancing and pulling back in order to seek and find their advantage. They make countless assaults too long to recount, and from morning until nones they have little or no rest.

The weather was at that time very hot. The knights became overheated, and there was no limb that was not in pain from this difficult work, and rightly so. Even those who were neither taking nor giving blows were worn out from seeing them do battle for so long in a single joust. Very hard did the two knights work. There is no means that they would not willingly use to vanquish each other, so they defended themselves and sought only to strike well and test their noble prowess and valiance in this high enterprise.

Now they would willingly rest, for this laborious effort indeed requires repose, but the hearts of these two knights did not deign to do so. First one, then the other gained on his opponent, but their high determination could not suffice to maintain this labor. They were forced to drop their shields because of all the blows, to lower their swords, and to wrestle with each other with all their might, fighting in such a way that each of them dropped on one knee. The big knight, marveling at finding such a strong opponent, was tired and bewildered. He had no more strength or power; he was out of breath; and Erec, whose good courage grew, drove the knight in such a way that he knocked him to the ground so badly wounded that he could no longer go on. Erec unlaced his helmet, telling him to ask for mercy or else he would promptly make his head fly.

[p. 205] 39. *How the young woman's champion recognized Erec's feat and begged for mercy*

When the knight saw that he was vanquished by the fine performance of the most worthy warrior Erec, he asked him to take pity on him and to tell him his name, 'so that', said he, 'I may die more happily if someone more noble than I has conquered me or more meanly if you are of less noble lineage than I.'

'My name will I tell you willingly,' said Erec, 'but it will be on condition that I learn the reason why you are guarding this orchard.' The knight promised to tell him the truth about it, and Erec proceeded to say, 'Sir knight, in order that you may not believe that you were defeated by a knight of lesser

---

[19] The syntax in this passage is tortured: a repetition of 'the third time' and 'the third course' and a complicated order render the sentence difficult to understand.

nobility, I respond that I am of royal lineage and am the son of the very high and noble King Lac, and my name is Erec.'

This knight of the orchard was overjoyed when he heard that his opponent was the son of King Lac. He told Erec that he once lived with his father, before becoming a knight. 'And to inform you about the adventure that keeps me in this orchard, may you know that the young lady you see there and I have loved each other since our earliest childhood. Because our love was ardent, she was happy to leave her country and come with me to this land. During our journey we found ourselves in this spot. At that time she wished to rest and implored me to grant a request without naming it. I agreed to it, as one who did not wish to refuse her anything, and she, inflamed with love for me, upon hearing the pledge I made to her in this very orchard, entreated me to never leave this spot until a knight vanquished me in armed combat. When he learned about this incident, my uncle, King Evrain, was deeply saddened. The young lady knows many arts[20] through which – or through gifts from fairies – she devises the good things in this pleasant place, where many noble knights have gathered, whom I conquered while keeping my promise. But since it has turned out [p. 206] that you have checkmated me in armed combat, I am quit and will depart with you, which will bring jubilation to each and every one, and this is the Joy of the Court that you will presently give to my uncle and his barons. And to inform you of my name, I am called Mabonagrein, completely ready to accomplish for you, and in your honor, what it pleases you to command.'

Then Erec raised up the knight and granted him mercy, and Mabonagrein led him to the horn, which Erec blew so loudly that the orchard resounded from it. Thereupon appeared among the king and the lords of the land the Joy of the Court. Thus at the moment when Erec blew the horn, you would have seen everyone, on foot or on horseback, enter the orchard, manifesting the greatest joy in the world. Enide was overjoyed by the exploit of her husband Erec, who was quickly disarmed by the noblest men of this kingdom, carrying on so noisily about this unaccustomed Joy of the Court that it seemed as if they had found a god on earth. Even the ladies, in remembrance of this happy day, created a lay, and there was no woman who did not give herself over to singing with a joyous heart.

Alas! The young lady and loyal friend of Mabonagrein, who is sitting on the silver bed, does not see what her heart desires, for contrary to the other ladies, within her descends a cold and pale sorrow that tears her entire heart out, and she is served more than one hundred melancholy thoughts.

Upon this new expression of joy, Enide looked sweetly at the young woman and recognized by her sad and sorrowful position that she was dejected and chagrined, so she turned to her in order to comfort her, along with other ladies desirous of giving hope to the woman who was deeply saddened by the commonly shared joy. From her eyes fell copious tears, because of an

---

[20] 'Sciences' in the text.

anguished remembrance, so much so that they took over her senses and judgment and made her lose countenance and bearing. Despite whatever sorrow she felt, upon seeing the ladies coming towards her, the young woman rose quickly and stood up; and Enide greeted her nobly as one who knew very well how to do so. To that the distressed and sad young lady could only respond with sighs and sobs that burst forth then and [p. 207] prevented her from speaking for a long time. When she stopped sighing, she returned Enide's greeting; and once she had looked at her for a little while, it seemed to her that she had seen her in the past, so she could not help asking with her very first words what country and region Enide was from. Gently, Enide replied that she was the daughter of the count of Lalut's sister.

At these words, the young lady, who shortly before had been overcome with excessive grief and affliction, became completely filled with delight and began to say, all the while smiling and hugging or kissing Enide, 'Alas! My most beloved cousin, may God be praised for your coming! You don't recognize me because you haven't seen me for a long time, but so that you may remember me, my lady, I tell you that I am the daughter of the count of Lalut, my lord father, may God watch over him and may his honor grow, he who once had a war to conduct against some of his enemies. In that war many noble knights participated; among them Mabonagrein carried himself very valiantly – so much so that everyone spoke only of his fine performance. Because of the reputation that everyone accorded to him, at his request and humble supplication, I granted him my love – for he wished to kill himself and despair if I did not love him. And because of the promise he made to always be loyal to me until death, and since I was certain that he was from a high rank and a good family, I was happy to leave my country and come with him to this land. Thanks be to God, I am not unhappy now about your arrival; instead, I am presently reaching the limits of bliss as much as I was earlier exceeding the limits of darkness and distress.'

At these words the two women kissed each other again, and soon the reunion was revealed to Erec, Guivret, and Mabonagrein, who went to recount it to the king. So you must know that never was more joyous acquaintance made, for through this reunion the lady of the orchard was completely comforted, and her grief turned to joy. Indeed, when she learned that her first cousin would soon be crowned as queen of a powerful kingdom, she knew not how to demonstrate enough her joyous state of mind.

[p. 208] 40. *How Erec went to King Arthur's court and learned the news that his father, the king, had died*

Finally, with great honor the young lady of Lalut was taken to Guivret and Erec's castle. There the marriage was celebrated between Mabonagrein and the damsel; and after the solemn wedding feast, which lasted two weeks, Erec took leave of King Evrain, of the damsel or lady of Mabonagrein, and indeed of all the princes of this region, and set off from there for Great

Britain, where King Arthur was. But you must know that Erec was nobly accompanied and that several men presented their service, in their person and possessions. As therefore Erec and Guivret had set forth on their way, they traveled until they arrived in London, where King Arthur, the queen, and the barons were. And as soon as the king heard about the arrival of Erec and Enide, we must say that he was very delighted. He went to meet Erec, welcoming him nobly, and Enide as well.

At court they stayed a long time, until news came that King Lac, Erec's father, had passed away two weeks earlier, in November. Erec, Enide, the king, and the queen grieved over this event and cried bitterly. But nevertheless, King Arthur, wishing to crown Erec as the heir in succession, sent for all his nobles for a day at Christmastide and with the greatest honor that can be done to a man, he crowned Erec and Enide. And the archbishop of Canterbury anointed them in the church in the palace of the city of London, where everyone was assembled on that day. And the story says that in order to heighten the solemnity of the festivities, King Arthur dressed four hundred knights in the same outfits and mounted them on coursers and chargers, and ordered a small tourney or bohort between two hundred knights against two hundred, who took up pennants and banners. And when King Erec learned about the tourney that was to take place, secretly he had black armor prepared, in which he fought. And he performed [p. 209] several valiant feats and acts of prowess that would be too long to recount, but we will pass some of them in review, briefly, as is the custom.

41. *How King Erec entered into the tourney and performed many chivalric exploits*

Thus, when Erec learned that the king and the ladies were at the lines of battle and that the knights had begun the tourney, he left a spot so secretly that no one noticed it. He entered the field and thrust himself where he saw the weakest side, for it seemed[21] it was being defeated through the high deeds of two knights, one of whom was Sir Gauvain and the other was Blioberis. Before them no one could stand, for they did nothing but marvels. At the time when King Erec arrived at the tourney, Sir Gauvain had taken a big lance and was catching his breath on the side. King Erec saw him upon arriving, and it seemed to him that the former had caught his breath well enough, so he took his spear, which his squire was carrying for him, and instantly came running like lightning against Sir Gauvain, who saw him coming, and by his bearing realized he was a knight who had proved his worth.

King Erec turned his horse's head in his direction and couched his lance, then the two knights came together and with all their strength, struck each other. Sir Gauvain broke his lance, and King Erec struck him with such force

---

[21] 'Seemed' inserted to fill a lacuna; see Foerster, p. 292, and Colombo Timelli, note, p. 217.

that he brought him from his horse to the ground. And on the very same attack he encountered Blioberis, who had seen Sir Gauvain fall. And with his spear, which was still whole, Erec struck Blioberis in such a way that he pierced his shield and hauberk and gave him a large wound in the left side, carrying him and his horse to the ground, turned out in such a way that he was indeed in need of a doctor. With that accomplished, he entered into the thickest press, and before breaking his spear, he did as much as a knight can [p. 210] do, for he brought low four or five knights. With his spear broken, he drew his sword and began to perform so many great deeds of knighthood that they cannot be described. He strikes down knights and horses, tears shields from around necks and helmets from heads; before his blows no man remains in the saddle, so much so that those who latterly were fleeing have recovered boldness through his good deeds, while those who were chasing them are so alarmed that they lose control. And when the heralds see the great exploits that Erec is going about doing and that everywhere he goes, he makes himself known, they begin crying out in unison, 'May honor be given to the knight in black armor who is vanquishing all!' And similarly, there where the king and the queens, knights, ladies, and damsels are, seeing all that is done on the field, they say they have never seen a knight do so many feats of arms, nor prove himself so passionately in a tournament. While everyone was praising and acclaiming this knight Erec, he continued on, from very well to better, and it did not seem that for an entire day he should stop his good deeds.

While he was performing truly marvelous exploits and everyone was afraid to encounter him, along came Sir Gauvain, who had picked himself up with great difficulty, for he was hurt from having fallen hard. Now he has recovered a lance; he looks at King Erec acquitting himself well, for he does not seem any more weakened than at the first blow. Thus he heads toward Erec, who sees him couch his lance and run forward so quickly that it seems he must fell him. Erec does not know what to say, for he has neither sword, spear, staff, nor lance. Nevertheless, he plucks all fear from his heart and gives free rein to his charger, which he feels is still strong and light, then steadies himself in his stirrups and hits the spurs, and comes as quickly as he can towards Sir Gauvain, who gives him such a blow in the middle of his shield that the lance flies to pieces but does not budge Erec from his saddle. And as Erec passed, he struck Sir Gauvain on his helmet with all his strength, so much so that because of the [p. 211] blow, which was great, he was so stunned that he lost his saddle-bows and stirrups and fell to the ground.

When King Erec saw himself delivered from Sir Gauvain, whom he did not recognize, he was overjoyed. He passed beyond and struck out again against those who were opposed to his side in such a way that he made himself so well known that everyone began to cry out, 'Flee, flee! Here comes the knight in black armor who fells everything. Against him we can no longer resist!' Then those in Sir Gauvain's party began to be put to rout. They turned their backs and have gone off, back to the battle lines in great fear, as if relinquishing the tournament.

42. *How Erec left King Arthur's court and went off to his kingdom*

When Erec saw that no one wished to continue the tourney, he left the field secretly, but he was unable to get away before King Arthur, who wished indeed to meet him, mounted his palfrey and came to him just as he thought he would go to his lodgings. The king enjoined him, on the thing he loved most in the world, to tell him his name. Thus enjoined, Erec revealed who he was, which made the king so joyful that never was a man more so. He made it known to the ladies, who honored Erec greatly upon his return and judged, according to their discernment, that he was the best knight in the world. Thus was Erec in the good graces of the ladies; and to make things brief, we will not mention the dinners, suppers, dances, and entertainments that were held during two weeks, for one can well enough know and understand that there were enough of them and that the entire nobility shared in them.

To conclude our tale, after the coronation ceremony, for which a great number of knights had assembled, King Erec and Queen Enide took leave of King Arthur and the queen, and a very noble company of high [p. 212] princes and barons escorted them all the way to their kingdom, where King Erec accepted homage and fealty from his nobles. And ever after he lived in a holy and glorious fashion with his beautiful lady, the queen Enide, who gave him many beautiful children; and once this progeniture had come of age, King Erec and Enide passed away from this world peacefully, and their funeral was held reverently with great tears on the part of their children, of whom the eldest became king. But our tale makes no further mention of these events; thus we will bring to an end this present story.

Explicit

THE BOOK OF ALIXANDRE, EMPEROR OF CONSTANTINOPLE,
AND HIS SON CLIGÉS

Translated by Joan Tasker Grimbert

Contents

The Book of Alixandre, Emperor of Constantinople, and His Son Cligés

[p. 65] However unworthy I am to apply my feeble intelligence to the current fashion of transposing the deeds of some nobles of old from verse to prose, nevertheless, knowing that my contemporaries are turning willingly to the good practice of reading and listening to romances and histories instead of indulging in pastimes, I shall venture to transpose the present account. Although I know my talent is insufficient to the task, I shall do this nonetheless in order to avoid sloth and in obedience to my most lofty and feared prince, praying that he and all others will excuse my ignorance and have patience with my coarse and plain language.

Here follows the story[1] of the noble and valiant emperor Cligés, which is told in two short parts, namely: the first contains the deeds of noble Alixandre, father of Cligés, and the second contains the memorable adventures of said Cligés, son of Soredamors.

> [p. 66] 1. *Here follows the first chapter of the brief account that relates to Alixandre, father of Cligés, starting with how Alixandre resolved to go serve King Arthur*

At the time the most noble and victorious King Arthur wore the crown of the kingdom of Great Britain, there reigned in Constantinople an emperor named Alixandre, who was a man of great prudence and possessed of fine qualities. His wife was a high lady of noble birth and royal lineage named Thantalis. So lovingly and in such harmony did they pass their time in this world that God granted the clever artisan Lady Nature permission to provide them with two sons: the first was called Alixandre, after his father, and the second, Alix. But Alixandre had already passed through all the stages of youth – childhood, boyhood, and adolescence – when Alix was procreated and come into the world.

Alixandre was well built in every respect, and upon reaching the age of reason, he developed to a lofty degree his noble and valorous spirit, demonstrating that he was descended from noble stock. He decided that he wished to pursue the noble exercise of arms and, seeing that in the Greek

---

[1] The adapter uses the term '(h)istoire' (= story) to refer to the source, whereas he uses 'compte' (= account) to refer to the adaptation (as in the title of chapter 1 below).

empire he could not very well engage in this noble trade, he told himself that he would depart and set out for the place where he might hear it said that arms were best practiced. But when he consulted several noble knights about this matter, they spoke only of King Arthur, who had the renown and reputation of this time because the best knights in the whole world assembled daily at his court.

[p. 67] 2. *How Alixandre obtained leave from the emperor to go to King Arthur's court*

Having ascertained from his inquiry that all the best knights in the world were in Great Britain at King Arthur's court, Alixandre went before his father the emperor and, after declaring his intention of going to Britain, employed such good means that he obtained leave from his father. In fact the emperor was very joyful because he knew well that his son, given his disposition, would manage to do great good some day. He had taught his son to be humble, courteous, obliging, and diligent in his endeavors, saying that if he could one day possess these qualities, they would raise him to the sovereign seat of worldly felicity and consequently to the glorious throne. 'And,' he said, 'because you are my son, so that you may make yourself worthy in the service you so ardently desire, I shall open up our treasury to you and put you in a position to draw on it for as much and as liberally as you think best.'

The noble emperor had barely finished his counsel when the empress Thantalis arrived, and upon hearing discussed the departure of her son Alixandre fainted straightaway. The emperor raised her up as soon as he could, comforting her and begging her to cease her mourning, but to no avail. For Maternal Love came before her, speaking covertly in this way, 'Poor unfortunate woman, what will become of you when your child leaves you and ventures, as he wishes, to follow the difficult path over the long, wide sea with its perilous waves?' Oh, what heaving sobs resonate in the heart of the noble Lady Thantalis at these words. She cannot control her behavior, and already the nature of the feminine sex inclines her to weep effusively over the distressing departure[2] of her son.

Seeing this, the emperor was very sad and, [p. 68] to give her hope, he ventured to say, 'Oh, my lady, you who weep piteously over your son's departure, take heart, if you are reasonable; for your son conducts himself with great wisdom, and his resolve to go to Arthur's court springs from a noble and good desire. With the help of God and Fortune, he will, upon arriving, be worthy of earning lofty praise, good, and honor, and you should derive great joy from having engendered such great valor. I do not wish to say, of course, that Maternal Love, upon seeing her son depart, must not

---

[2] 'departure': for a lacuna that occurs here, Foerster, p. 352, proposed 'departie'. See also Colombo Timelli, p. 166.

have her say, with effusive sighs, tears, and pleas that he remain. For this reason, you must bear this voyage as best you can, for since the resolution has been taken, I must say that if he tarried, the delay would signal a heart that is very faint, simple, and indolent, despite the genuine love he has for you.' Little by little the lady became reconciled; and noble Alixandre had his ships filled and loaded with all he needed.

3. How Alixandre left Constantinople with great regret

Early the next day, Alixandre, ardently desiring to be on his way[3] and to receive the order of chivalry from the hand of King Arthur, had his barons get ready, then he went to his father the emperor and his mother Thantalis, who was weeping tenderly at his leave-taking. You should have seen how on uttering the word 'adieu', there appeared a sweet and gracious tear stemming from the genuine love that the son felt for the father and also the father and the mother for the son. And because the departure had to take place, they were able only with much difficulty to exchange that word. For the emperor and the lady were quite distressed[4] at having to bid adieu to their child who was leaving. Nevertheless, they [p. 69] accompanied him with great weeping as far as the sea's shore. They saw that the water was calm and peaceful, so they conceived good hope and said more than a hundred thousand times, 'Adieu, my son, adieu, my son.' And with the last 'adieu' Thantalis hugged and kissed her son, and finally he left her and turned in the direction of his ship with the greatest regret in the world. He found his sailors ready, and as soon as he had boarded the ship they spread full the sails and weighed anchor, and then rowing joyfully receded from the shore and went sailing along like men well served by the wind. The emperor and Thantalis followed them with their eyes as far as they could, asking God to grant them success.

Now, our account will fall silent regarding the emperor and Thantalis and proceed to recount the deeds of Alixandre, who with ardent desire sailed over the sea toward Great Britain.

4. How Alixandre arrived at the port of Southampton and went to speak to King Arthur

The story recounts that when Alixandre had already navigated the sea's treacherous currents, and they had already traveled for several days and nights, Good Fortune led him to the port of Southampton, and Alixandre's

---

[3] 'on his way': proposed to fill a lacuna recorded by Colombo Timelli, p. 68. She notes, p. 166, that Foerster's text shows no lacuna at p. 285.

[4] 'distressed': proposed to fill a lacuna recorded by Colombo Timelli, p. 68. Foerster's text shows the lacuna at p. 285 but leaves it blank.

squires, who were ill[5] from breathing sea air, to which they were not at all accustomed, were very joyful. And whereas shortly before they had been sad and gloomy from their long and tedious voyage, as soon as they set foot on land they were cured and forgot all about their travails. In short, Alixandre with his noble company of knights entered Southampton where they rejoiced greatly. But he did not forget to inquire as to where King Arthur was holding court, for it was the first thing that he ever asked, and he learned that the king was very close by in a city named Winchester. [p. 70] In this city of Southampton Alixandre took lodging that night and rejoiced greatly, praising God that he had arrived so safely, and he decided that the next day he would achieve his goal. He did so, for the next morning he left Southampton and made such good time that around the hour of tierce[6] he found himself in Winchester and took lodging with a townsman; then he donned his best clothes and went off to where the king was. Alixandre approached and greeted him, and his squires did likewise.

King Arthur, crowned and seated on his royal throne, saw and gazed at these noble young men of Greece, and from all of them he singled out Alixandre for his beauty. He rejoiced upon seeing them and, when he had received their greetings, he asked them what they wanted and needed. Alixandre answered, 'In truth, lord king, because your lofty excellence is known all over the world, and because there are no chivalric deeds accomplished except by the knights of your Round Table, since I wish to learn the noble and fine trade of arms, I have humbly undertaken to come serve you if you would have me. For my principal wish and the one thing in the world that I most desire is to be considered one day a knight of your retinue.'

'Fair son,' said the king, 'I am very happy that you have come, and be assured that I would be more than chagrined if I did not want to accept the service of a youth as handsome as you. For your stature indicates clearly that you come from good family and that nobility reigns in your heart and governs your fair body, which is more handsome than any I have seen in a long time. But before you do enter my service, I beg you to tell me your name, country, and from what regions you have come here.'

'It is quite right that I should tell you, Sire,' said Alixandre. 'I am a native of Constantinople, elder son of my lord and father the emperor, and my name is Alixandre.'

'I should certainly rejoice greatly over the arrival of such a squire,' said the king, 'and it seems to me that you truly do me great honor when by your humility you [p. 71] come to serve a lesser person than yourself.'

Then he approached Alixandre and raised him up, saying, 'Fair friend, you are most welcome here. If it should please God, you will lose nothing by coming: learn and you will act wisely.' Hearing these words, the other

---

[5] 'ill': proposed to fill a lacuna that Foerster shows at p. 285 but leaves blank. Colombo Timelli, p. 166, cites the corresponding text in Chrétien's *Cligés* (ed. Gregory and Luttrell, vv. 280–3), which states that the men were weak and sick.

[6] See the glossary for this and other terms pertaining to medieval culture.

Greeks stood up, very pleased to see that the king deigned to welcome their master Alixandre, who of the other knights at court was greatly feted and honored. And indeed, on welcoming this noble squire, they jousted, danced, and played many games. And because my lord Gauvain found him pleasant and debonair, he often kept him company,[7] as did several others, and because of the good words and gracious ways with which he dealt with his elders, Alixandre was never without the company of several knights of the court.

5. *How King Arthur departed for Brittany,* *leaving the count of Windsor in charge of his kingdom*

Alixandre conducted himself with increasing honor in King Arthur's court. He had a great deal of money and, because he wished to act in a way befitting an emperor's son, he made numerous gifts, so many that no one could say enough good about him. For he was not stingy with gold or silver; rather, he spent generously as his station allowed him, indeed so generously that all marveled at the noble life he led. Consequently, the king was very happy with him, as was the queen.

Alixandre had been at the king's court for a long time without encountering any adventures worth recounting when Arthur one day felt the urge to go seek diversion in Brittany. He assembled his barons and in accordance with their will entrusted Great Britain to the count of Windsor until his return. Then he took to sea in the company only of the queen, Soredamors, and Alixandre, for there were no other knights in the king's boat. But you must know that in the other ships there was a fine company of knights and many ladies and maidens. The sails were spread to their fullest, and [p. 72] finally the sailors set out to sea and in a short time were well advanced.

6. *How Alixandre and Soredamors were* *struck with love for each other*

As you have heard, King Arthur departed abruptly from England, which was then called Great Britain, taking with him the queen and Soredamors, sister of the noble and valiant knight Sir Gauvain. May God guide them. This voyage was to give rise to a very great good: for a lady who had never before deigned to love any knight or squire, no matter how courageous or valiant, on that day was subdued by Love and caught in his bonds as a result of a novel transformation.

The beautiful maiden of whom our account makes mention, namely Soredamors, is seated directly opposite Alixandre in the boat and is forced to look at him, whether she wants to or not. And because she notices that he

---

[7] 'he often kept him company': roughly the meaning proposed by Foerster, p. 352, to fill a lacuna. See also Colombo Timelli, p. 167.

is so handsome and polite, she is forced to recognize and admit to herself
that his beauty surpasses that of the handsomest men in the world. Then
Love strikes her with his gilded arrow, indeed, right in the middle of her
heart, and, on being wounded, she changes color several times. In no way
can she keep from looking at Alixandre, and she has to pay in one fell
swoop for having refused many noble men. The artless intelligence of this
young lady, who was once so stubborn in her contempt for men, is, by a
sudden ray of Love's powers, made vulnerable and a slave at the sight of
Alixandre's beauty.

So you must know that in order to root out that accursed obstinacy that
Soredamors had toward noble men, Love was obliged to reveal clearly his
powers, [p.73] as he did. For although the maiden's heart was inured and
resistant to Nature's desires, to Love's commandments and summons, and
even to Reason, since she believed that no man was adequate to obtain her
good grace, nevertheless she was overwhelmed by this ray that descended
from the sun in Love's sky. And to the degree that she had been rebellious
and disdainful about loving anyone, to that same degree and more was
she desirous of love and determined in her resolve that she would be very
happy if such a squire wished to incline his love toward her, though in many
ways she did not deny that she would defend herself against the assaults
that Love was waging on her. For I shall never say that she did not conduct
herself very well during the battles that Love and Pride waged against each
other within her.

7. How Alixandre was exhorted to love the maiden Soredamors

If Soredamors is extremely pensive and melancholy, Alixandre is no less so.
He sees incessantly this beautiful young lady and, as he is reflecting on her
beauty, Love strikes him and begins instantly to offer this counsel: 'My son,
just look at the sweetest creature alive. You are handsome and well built, and
it seems to me that you would be very fortunate if you could obtain so great
a good as to possess the most beautiful of the beautiful.' There is no need
to inquire how Alixandre reacts when he hears Love's counsel. He sets his
mind on admiring the courtly demeanor of this fine and noble maiden and
does not cease to emit sighs and sobs corresponding to those of the woman
who loves him.[8] This love is very loyal and emanates [p. 74] from a solid
foundation and an amorous light, such that Soredamors is not deceived,
nor is Alixandre. For in an instant loyalty cannot have occupied a greater
place in the hearts of two lovers without their knowing each other's will.
But although they do not say a word to each other, their behavior reveals

---

[8]   As Colombo Timelli, p. 167, observes, the Middle French is ambiguous: the phrase could
be translated as either 'who loves him' ('celle qui l'ayme') or 'whom he loves' ('celle qu'il
ayme'). In her edition, she has chosen the first option, which we have adopted.

a great deal about their thoughts, and whoever might be attentive to their actions could clearly conceive in this case of their painful malady.

8. How King Arthur arrived at the port of Brittany, and Soredamors's behavior is described

Soredamors and Alixandre gazed at each other so much that the noble Queen Guenevere perceived to some extent that their sweet gazes were transmitting the messages and embassies of Love, for she saw them tremble and often grow pale and blush. She said nothing, but she understood very well. And of the two lovers she blamed neither, for she would be very pleased if they came together, and truly believed that they had spoken together previously, whereas they had not.

And thus the king's company progressed through the various depths and arms of the sea, sailing along rapidly until they arrived at the port of Brittany. The king set foot on land, and the people escorted him with great joy to one of his castles, where he took his pleasure for several days hunting and hawking. But since these activities do not pertain to our matter, we will leave them aside and now speak about Soredamors and Alixandre, who think so much about each other that they are unable to sleep night or day.

[p. 75] 9. How Alixandre speaks to himself and debates in his heart on the subject of his love

The story tells that from hour to hour Alixandre, who does honor and homage to the high god of Love, reflects and debates in his noble heart on the most excellent beauty of the lady who sighs for love of him. But now shame and fear prevent him from revealing his anguish to anyone, and especially to the one who has stolen his heart – she, who as his sovereign doctor can, by a single word of hope, allay and bear the greatest part of his suffering.

The same emotions are harbored by the beautiful maiden Soredamors. The two lovers cannot bear to speak to one another, but, since they do not know what else to do, they turn their eyes and gaze tenderly at each other with a sweet impulse that encourages their two hearts to maintain and persevere in the continuation of their endeavors. And when night comes, and they cannot see each other, then their minds are oppressed by various dreams of love and melancholy thoughts. And in fact Alixandre, though he believes he is resting in his bed, cannot do so, for he is constrained, as one burning with desire to see his beloved, to reflect on her beauty, which seems to him so well inscribed in him that he cannot forget it.

And when he considers his situation and realizes that he dares not speak to her, he calls himself a fool, saying, 'Poor foolish man, what do you want to do if you dare not reveal your torment? Do you want to languish incessantly in miserable pain since you have neither the courage nor the boldness to ask for succor from this grievous malady that can only be relieved by the mercy of the most beautiful woman in the world – and indeed who in my opinion surpasses all the beauty with which women can be endowed? Oh, how unfortunate and cowardly is he who, too indolent to ask for relief, cannot obtain help for what grieves him! Clearly, I labor in vain if I dare not ask for a word with the one [p. 76] who by one sweet word in simple response can relieve my infirmity and my cursed affliction, which is so dreadful to cure that no herb, unguent, root, or liquor could suffice. And whoever considers well Love's malady knows it is harder to bear than any other; for I am sure that, if Love does not favor me and soon take pity and compassion on my heart, it could be battered for lack of the gracious medicine that it ardently desires because of Love, who wishes it thus. And for this reason, I shall complain about Love and the remedy for the wound he has made in me, his very loyal servant, since only a single person can comfort me, indeed in accordance with his commandment. For, since I was content a short time ago to obey his will, it was in the hope of improving my situation, believing that in Love's service I should have only pleasure and joy. But, on the contrary, instead of this most desired enjoyment, I am assailed with all the painful torments with which Fortune can torment the heart of a young man in this situation.

'No one who has not experienced it knows what it is to love, and, so help me God, if I had thought, upon first looking at the beautiful maiden, that because of this single look I would be caught up in this painful affliction, I would have instead cast my eyes aside, against their will, if it had been possible, in order to avoid this danger. And I do believe I would be very sensible if I no longer thought about her, but I don't know how I can do that, for Love wishes perhaps to chastise me and demonstrate his power over me at this moment of my initiation. And I do believe that Love, who is a fair judge, will, after this grievous suffering, help to console my heart, which he has pierced through with his dart.

'Pierced through? What am I saying? How can that be, for the wound is not visible from the outside? Could he have sent the dart through the eye? Certainly not, for my eye would have been poked out, and thanks be to God, it is whole and healthy, so it is impossible that the dart was directed there. Consequently, [p. 77] I am very surprised and would like to know how Love wounded my heart so very cruelly without making a visible wound on my body.'

At these words, there came before Alixandre a Counsel, saying, 'My fair son who inquires how Love can have struck you in the heart, know that his ways are so subtle that they are not to be made manifest at first blush. And know that, when first you cast your eyes on Soredamors, and she seemed beautiful to you, then Love looked at you from atop his high imperial throne and cast into the midst of your thoughts the arrow that entered your heart without wounding your body, just as the sun passes through glass without breaking it. And for this reason, you should never give this pause or waste your time on it, for it would be better if you found a way and manner of obtaining the good grace of the one for whom your heart daily heaves sighs and sobs by the hundreds and thousands.' After this, Alixandre does not know what to say. He imagines and considers how he might have a word with his beloved and resolves to wait for Love to provide for it and the young lady's favor.

10. *How Soredamors reflected on Alixandre's attractions*

If Alixandre was extremely ill at ease in this beginning phase, the maiden Soredamors was no less so. She was barely able to sleep, for Love had imprisoned and enclosed her heart so securely that she sighed, trembled, and was so afflicted with an abundance of thoughts that she could scarcely catch her breath. So she took to complaining in this manner: 'Oh, woe is me, how foolish and silly I am to reflect on Alixandre's powerful attractions; for if he is beautiful and of good birth, he is not for me, and I would not be wise to love him, since he surpasses all men in beauty, knowledge, and courtesy. And for that reason [p. 78] I would be wrong to hate him, and even if my body wanted to do so, my heart would not allow it, although I do not love him or anyone else. And if I cannot help inscribing his sweet gaze in my heart, then I would have to say that this is Love, for my eye would never turn to admire his sweet and powerful attractions if I were not in love with him. For, although I wish I could rest and cease thinking about him, I cannot do so, for Love has invaded me so cruelly, and I have to moderate my will and accede to Love's unexpected commandments which I have so long opposed and resisted that I can no longer do so. I must surrender and do what Love tells me, namely, be receptive to the most amiable young man under heaven; and moreover Love wants me to be loving, loyal, courteous, and obedient. Thus, if I do not want to be considered haughty, proud, rebellious, and totally ungracious, I must soften my heart and turn my eyes often toward the beauty that is my desire. And since Reason declares that I must for once do my duty toward Love, I shall do what my name teaches me. For "sore" signifies the color of gold, which is the most golden and most pure; and the other part, "d'amors", joined to the first word "sore", must be equivalent to "sororee d'amours", that is to say, the woman the most intimate with Love's ways that ever existed. I do not stray much from acting reasonably if I do what my name signifies, and therefore I shall never desist from loving the man I can best serve all my life. And if it were not for Fear which comes before me, I would say that I should declare myself, but upon my faith I would be too immodest if I requested what others have requested of me and to which I was never inclined to consent despite any supplications whatsoever. May God keep me from committing a fault, and in truth ladies will never reproach me [p. 79] if I believe that Fortune will not increase so much my suffering that I should have to request a man's love.'

11. *What King Arthur did to the count of Windsor,*
who wanted to rebel against him

When Soredamors had said these words in her heart and saw Love who assailed her thus with all his might, you need not ask what hallucinations enveloped her. She could not rest, and the most sensible thing she could do was to debate with herself saying, 'Oh, how poor is my noble and loyal heart, since it does not cease its sighs with harsh and painful thoughts because of a single ray from Love's hot and ardent sun, which Love caused to shine and spread over me. Thus, so help me God, I shall show my beloved such a countenance that if he is not as hard as stone, he will try to request my love. For if Love, by means of a sudden desire born in the heart's fountain, strikes him once deeply, it will make him advance and by a curious accord seek incessantly to be in my good grace, through the faith and loyalty that he will promise me. I really do not know what his desire is', she said, 'but in any case I pray to God that He should wish to help me as well as He can, for I truly need it.'

The two lovers were occupied a long time debating with themselves. But after King Arthur had spent about four to five months traveling around various castles, towns, and fortresses, there came messengers from London and Canterbury who told the king in very dreadful terms that the count of Windsor, whom he had left in charge of Great Britain, had assembled a large number of men-at-arms and had set himself up in the city of London saying that he would be lord and master of it and would keep and hold the town against all. The king marveled greatly at this news and, most upset, he very angrily summoned his barons and, [p. 80] in order to motivate them to avenge his subjects' rebellion, he told them they had erred in advising him to leave his land in the care of a rebellious, false, and treacherous evildoer who wished to hold sway over something of which he was not even worthy to be a servant.

At these words, the men of Brittany and many other regions swore they would avenge him; never would they rest until the criminal had been punished. Owing to these promises, the king conceived great hope and made it known throughout Gaul that every man should respond to this order by taking up arms to help him against his subjects in Great Britain who wanted to rebel against him. And you must know that on the day they heard this, all the knights of Gaul, which is now called France, departed and came together in Brittany at the court of King Arthur who, seeing his army ready and his ships prepared, departed along with his queen and all his barons and set out to sea in great splendor, yearning to take vengeance against his enemy.

12. *How the queen gave Alixandre a chemise*

When Alixandre saw such a great assembly that everyone seemed to be there, he said he wanted to be knighted. He summoned his Greek compatriots and, with his heart overflowing with joy for the great desire that exalted it, he came before King Arthur saying, 'Sir, since I have entered your service to learn and obtain from your hand the rank of knighthood, I beg that it may please you by your grace to dub me if I deserve it, and may God grant that this be for my honor and your profit.' To which the king answered that he would willingly make him a knight and all those of his retinue as well. Then they all donned armor, shields, helmets, and hauberks. The king knighted them and girded their swords [p. 81] starting with the noble knight Alixandre who looked well suited to bear his arms. This event made the Greeks very joyful. They bathed in the sea for lack of other bath facilities. And Queen Guenevere, who loved Alixandre with a loyal love, took from a small chest a beautiful and expensive white chemise, all of silk, that Soredamors had stitched with gold thread, intertwining a strand of her hair with the thread in order to learn which was more resistant, the gold thread or the hair. The queen sent this chemise to Alixandre who received it with great joy and donned it after he had enjoyed his bath in the sea. Then, when he was fully dressed, he went over to where the king and queen were. God knows how well he showed them respect and thanked the queen gently for her courtesy.

But regarding these matters our account will fall silent, leaving Alixandre to reflect on his lady, and Soredamors on her beloved; it reports that King Arthur made such good progress over the sea that he arrived before the city of London.

13. *How the count of Windsor stole off by night from the city of London*

The story recounts then in this part that the peasants from around the perimeter of the city of London, seeing that their king had already arrived at the port with a great army, went to surrender to him armed and mounted to the best of their ability, some well and some less so, which made the king very happy, and he swore to himself never to leave until he has taken the city of London by love or by force.

The count of Windsor has gone up to a palace window and sees the great army, which frightens him, and he sees clearly that he will have to flee or die. Now he has to find the means to save his life. He assembles his accomplices and accepts their counsel that at nightfall, with daylight failing, [p. 82] he will take all the treasures from London and steal off secretly that night with a great number of traitors and flee to his castle in Windsor, which he has well fortified with outer walls and all other things. Once inside, he raises the drawbridge, and says then that he is secure and unconcerned about the king or anyone else. For while the king was in Brittany, the count, having charge of the great treasures, melted them down and built on that spot a castle[9] atop a very stable rock. All who wished to

---

[9] 'a castle': proposed by Foerster, pp. 292 and 352, to fill a lacuna. See Colombo Timelli, p. 170.

work on it were welcomed there to finish the project whose triple walls were surrounded by deep moats, and the sea[10] beat against the outer wall. And even when only the lower courtyard was in place, it seemed impregnable by assault or force.

14. How the people of the city of London begged for mercy from King Arthur, who went off to lay siege to Windsor Castle

The next day, the people of London got up in the morning and, seeing that those comprising the false garrison of the traitor, the count of Windsor, had fled for fear, they were very joyful, and of common accord they went bare-headed and without any arms to beg mercy, excusing themselves by claiming that the traitor had subjugated them by the violence of force and tried to dominate them and moreover had taxed them and made them pay a great sum of deniers.

The king took mercy on his people and, when he was sure that his enemy was in the castle at Windsor, he set out and continued along his path until he arrived at the port. He saw the place well protected, equipped with deep moats and artillery machines, and he knew full well that it could not be taken on the first try. He had his host stop there. Then you would have seen them setting up and preparing tents of every color – green, indigo, crimson, white, dark blue, and others – such that it is a noble thing to see the sun's rays on them, making them shine and [p. 83] sparkle over a space of more than a league in length.

Those in the castle truly believe they are secure. Pride takes hold of them and, as they suspect nothing, they issue from the castle mounted on good horses and each equipped with shield and lance alone and, because they want to show King Arthur that they do not fear his intelligence, force, or great host of knights, they leap and pirouette on the gravel as if wishing to amuse themselves.[11]

15. How Alixandre fights against those in the castle and kills many

The traitors have not yet all issued from the castle when Alixandre, on seeing them, stops and tells his men that by putting himself to the test, he wants to gauge their strength and boldness so he can gain renown and prove that he is full of nobility and possesses a strong will. He has himself

---

[10] Colombo Timelli, p. 170, suggests that the reference to 'sea' stems from an erroneous interpretation of 'Tamise' (= Thames) in Chrétien's *Cligés* (v. 1257).

[11] Between the end of this chapter and the beginning of the next, the scribe left a blank space equivalent to seven lines. It is one of several blank spaces in the manuscript that were presumably intended for the illuminator.

armed, and his companions likewise, saying, 'Now quickly, my knights! At this hour our actions must demonstrate our courage to these rebels who consider us so fainthearted that they have come unarmed to disport themselves before us. Oh, what great presumption moves them!' says Alixandre. 'Let us go use our lances, swords, and shields against them and prove our worth with the first advance, for we have the time and space.'

With these words Alixandre and his knights mount their good steeds and, when they see that they are quite ready, they show themselves and spur their horses to run toward the count of Windsor's men, who, as foolish as they are, do not flee but rather lower their lances and on both sides proceed [p. 84] to joust in such a way that every one of the Greeks unhorses his adversary, causing him to fall to the ground. The knights from the castle are all distraught when they see the strongest of their men felled with one blow of a lance. They turn their backs intending to go fetch their arms, but it is too late for some. Alixandre and his retinue pursue them relentlessly and kill them with their sword blades without much effort, for the men of Windsor, who thought a short time before that they would work marvels, do not know how to protect themselves except by running up to the castle as fast as they can. Most of them do not make it; rather, as many as a third are overtaken and killed, and the rest are followed up to the castle gate without a single man daring to appear before them, if not for his misfortune.

Alixandre captured four of the most confident knights from among the others, and returned to the king and queen with honor and praise from this skirmish. They had clearly seen him fight, and they received him with great joy and feted him with high pomp along with those of his rank. And Alixandre knelt humbly before the queen and presented her with the spoils from his first knightly exploit, namely, the four prisoners. But you should know that all those in the army prized Alixandre and praised him, except the king, who said not a word because he was distressed not to have the prisoners so he could put them to death. He asked the queen for them, and she gave them to him.

While they were being placed in chains, the queen led Alixandre, who had already disarmed, to the maidens' tent. He went inside, and in response to all the greetings performed his duty splendidly, then sat down next to Soredamors gazing sweetly at her, blushing and changing color [p. 85] often. And because he was very warm, he took off all the garments that were over the silk chemise that the queen had given him, then supported his head on his hand and lowered his face pensively. Soredamors, who was looking at him, was very distressed that he did not say anything to her. She recognized the chemise that he had put on from the strand of hair she had sewn into it so she would not mistake it, and it shone more than the gold. She said to herself, 'You are most fortunate, chemise, to adorn and be worn by the most refined knight in the world.' She stood up and walked about a little; then, as if love-struck, came to sit down next to Alixandre, reflecting on what would be the first word she would say to him. So she debated with herself if she would call him by his name, or rather, 'Beloved'.[12] 'This word "beloved" is the sweetest word I know, and if I dared call him "beloved", the word would be beautiful, but I fear it would be a lie; so I would be very sorrowful if I used it, for he is worthy to be called by his proper name. And yet I do not know if he loves me, even though for my part I would not be lying, and also he would not be wrong if he called me "beloved". The name Alixandre is a long one for a maiden to utter, and for this reason, upon my soul, I would prefer if his name were "beloved", truly, even if it were to cost me most of the blood in my body.'

While Soredamors was reflecting thus, Alixandre went to see the king, who greeted him warmly and ordered two knights to be brought to him, promising that he would grant him several good things if he persevered at length just as he had begun. Then he gave him the two knights that he wanted him to have, and, moreover, gave him five hundred archers and as many men-at-arms. Alixandre thanked the king one hundred thousand times, then departed and put his affairs in order so that if he were needed, he would be ready at all times.[13]

[p. 86] 16. *How the castle was besieged, and how the four prisoners were quartered using seven horses*

The very next day, the king wished to lay siege to the castle and had it announced that everyone should arm. You should have seen the knights arm themselves and the archers grab their quivers and their good bows, and elsewhere[14] servants saddle up the chargers and steeds that these men-at-arms mounted. Once they are ready and totally armed to begin battle, the king has them approach the castle, but he does not forget his prisoners. They make a great deal of noise as they move along. Those in the castle take notice and likewise ready themselves, and they put in front the artillerymen who, on the army's approach, fire cannons, bombards, coulovrines, crapaudeaux, veuglaires, and Greek fire. Even the archers and crossbowmen bend their bows and send forth volleys of arrows and all types of attack material so profusely that there is no[15] one so bold as to approach, and there is honor in going forward.

---

[12] The word 'ami(e)' in French is ambiguous: it means both 'friend' and 'beloved'. The following passage seems somewhat tortured, which reflects Soredamors's state of mind. There seem to be two issues here. One is that although calling him 'beloved' would reflect *her* feelings about him, she is not sure that it would reflect *his* feelings about her (in which case it would be a 'lie'). The second is that she thinks she should call him by his proper name but finds it too long to utter easily.

[13] Between the end of this chapter and the beginning of the next, the scribe left a blank space equivalent to eleven lines, presumably intended for the illuminator.

[14] 'elsewhere': Foerster, p. 295, proposed filling the lacuna after 'd'aultre' with 'part'. See Colombo Timelli, p. 171.

[15] 'there is no': I follow Colombo Timelli, p. 171, who proposes 'il n'y a' for the lacuna, which Foerster, p. 295, recognized but left blank.

Nevertheless, the king has the four prisoners brought before him and orders that they be attached to the tails of horses by their hands and feet, and then in this position dragged until death ensues. The executioner seizes them and attaches them as described above. And once they are bound, he chases the horses into the distance, and they all gallop off through mountains, rocks, thistles, brambles, nettles, and thorns, until the four evil men were put to death and so disfigured that not a single one of their limbs remained whole. Through an opening the count of Windsor sees them die and in great awe points them out to his accomplices, saying that King Arthur is very cruel, and that if they do not defend themselves they will be treated no less harshly. So they set out, and it seems that they do so willingly.

King Arthur finally approaches the castle, and with copper barrels and boats he manages to get a great number of his men [p. 87] over the moats to set foot at the bottom of the outer wall. Then the assault begins anew even more aggressively. Those on the outside raise ladders, and those on the inside use iron forks to knock the ladders down into the moats, carrying some of the men with them. You would have seen a fine assault, for you would not have been able to hear God thunder: it seemed as though the sky would burst open. Foot soldiers arrive and use large picks to break down the outer wall as best they can, but they do not have the strength to damage it, for the walls are built of thick, dark stone and are so well defended that never was there seen a finer assault. For those inside were throwing large stones from the battlements, and even the women brought water, oil, tar, and boiling hot ashes. And from the great, machicolated towers they hurled and shot out darts, javelins, cannons, arrows, crossbow bolts, and all other things you can imagine to make an assault and a defense. For those inside fear losing their lives and, because they have provisions, they defend themselves so bravely that all you can see are round and square stones falling and landing as thick as rain. In this way, those in the castle defend themselves against their assailants who persevere all day until surprised by nightfall when they have to take leave. Arthur sounds the retreat, and when he gets back he has it announced with the blast of a trumpet that the next day he will give a golden cup to the one who performs the finest exploit during the assault, and also, if he is a knight, he could never ask for anything that would not be granted to him except the king's crown and anything pertaining to his honor; no other exceptions would be made.

[p. 88] 17. *How the queen spoke to Soredamors about Alixandre's
chemise*

Before the proclamation was made, Alixandre went to see the queen, as was his custom, and after he had paid his respects to her, the queen took him by the hand and had him sit beside her. Soredamors was sitting on the other side and gazed willingly at Alixandre. The queen, seeing the strand of Soredamors's hair stitched into Alixandre's chemise, began to laugh softly, which made Alixandre uncomfortable, and he asked his lady and queen to tell him, if it was worth telling, why she was laughing. The queen summoned Soredamors, who came and knelt graciously before her, and Alixandre, who saw her approaching him, was so embarrassed that he dared not look at her. But you should know that Soredamors was even more discomfited than Alixandre. The queen saw how the two lovers were behaving at this point and, seeing them change color so often, she attributed this behavior to Love. She pretended not to perceive their malady, and in the end, as soon as Soredamors had stood up, the queen asked her if she had any idea where the chemise that the knight Alixandre was wearing had been made. The young lady was even more embarrassed than before. She finally admitted that she herself had sewn the chemise using a strand of her hair, but she apologized, saying it was unfortunate and accidental.

18. *How Alixandre slept with his chemise in his arms*

Upon hearing these words, Alixandre was suddenly filled with joy. He did not know what to do, and he could barely keep from kissing the chemise in front of everyone. Finally, like a man who does not know what he should do, he soon departed, taking leave of the queen and all the ladies. And [p. 89] when he was in a secluded spot, he took off the chemise and kissed and embraced it a thousand times, and even slept with it in his arms that night, saying that he was the most fortunate knight in the world.

At this point our account will fall silent with Alixandre thanking the gods and goddesses for the strand of Soredamors's hair that he had, and now it will speak about the traitors of Windsor, who spent all night dreaming and imagining how and in what way they could bring King Arthur's men to grief.

19. *How the men of Windsor resolved to attack their enemies by night*

The story recounts that, after the first attack had passed and was finished, the count of Windsor (may God punish him for his sins!) assembled his men and decided with his accomplices that he would sally forth secretly against his enemies at a fixed hour, namely, at three hours after midnight, when he believed he would find the king and his army asleep and unarmed: he was hoping thus to bring about such a massacre that it would be recounted forever after. It was done as he had resolved. All those in the castle armed themselves, then, at around daybreak, they went out and by the commandment of God, who rightly harms sinners, the sky became light a good hour and a half earlier than is usual in the course of nature. The sentries of the army glimpsed in the distance their enemies' armor, which was bright and fine, and they rushed to the knights' tents crying, 'To arms, get up, noble knights, quickly, for your enemies are coming this way in great force to surprise and harm you by this ruse!'

At these words, everyone sprang up as was necessary. They donned their armor and mounted their horses, while the traitors, [p. 90] who were divided into several parts, approached, hoping to accomplish their end, like men who believed they could attack King Arthur's army without any resistance. But God prevented them, for when they were in a good position to begin their attack, the king's party lined up and with a great company of men went forward to meet them.[16]

20. *How Windsor's men fought against King Arthur's army*

God, how bewildered were those from the castle when they saw their enemies! They did not deign to flee, but rather, like desperate men, risked their lives. They couched their good lances and went to meet the Britons, who rushed at them with such force that several fell on the ground to one side and the other. For the Britons seemed like starving lions pursuing their prey, and there was no one they reached who was not cut down in such a way that the wounds were not mortal and death did not ensue.

King Arthur was not at this first attack, nor were most of his knights, but Alixandre was among the first, and he accomplished such marvels and proved himself so well that day that he would be worthy to receive the golden cup. And when it came to seizing their swords, God knows how each strove to fight well. The traitors attacked with ardor, and those of the army defended themselves so nobly that their work was sufficient, for they killed more than five hundred of their enemies in less than a quarter of an hour. Among the others, Alixandre proved himself well: he ran out repeatedly, rushing [p. 91] and striking in the thickest part of the fray, and there where he saw that the enemy was dealing the hardest blows, he directed his efforts in such a way that nothing could resist him. He found a knight bearing indigo arms capering about and causing the battle lines to tremble all around him, and he wanted very much to test him. So he approached him and in the guise of a greeting struck a sword blow to his shoulder with such force that he severed it from his body and left his head dangling, then sent him sprawling to the ground dead.

Next, he looked farther ahead to see if he could find some feat to accomplish, and in fact a knight came up from behind and struck him on the helmet with his sword, because he had seen him kill the knight with the indigo arms. When Alixandre felt this blow, he turned around and rushed suddenly at the one who had struck him; he attacked him with such force that in striking he made him fall so rudely on his head that he broke his neck, and his horse landed on top of him. After these exploits, Alixandre

---

[16] Between the end of this chapter and the beginning of the next, the scribe left a blank space equivalent to about ten lines, presumably intended for the illuminator.

saw the treacherous count's seneschal performing great acts of chivalry. He
was not very pleased, and because he wanted to make the man pay for doing so well, and seeing that he would first have to pass through more than
five hundred traitors, he summoned his inner strength and, exerting himself,
he first spurred his steed into the thick[17] of the fray, rushing like a tempest,
striking and hitting so violently that there was not a man who did not clear
a path before him until he came to the seneschal who was waiting for him,
thinking he would defeat and kill him. Alixandre raised his sword and struck
the traitor on his helmet, but the blow landed obliquely. The seneschal did
not miss his mark, and he thought he would strike him from above, but
Alixandre, covering himself with his shield, dealt another sword blow that
sliced off half of the seneschal's collar along with his armor and unhorsed
him. Then more than a hundred archers surrounded Alixandre and assailed
him so brutally with their arrows that they slew his horse right under him.
Then they let out a loud cry that Sir Gauvain heard well. He came running
with all haste, and [p. 92] when he saw the good knight Alixandre standing
up to so many archers, he risked his life and did not stop striking until he
had helped him remount onto the best horse in the area.

21. *How Alixandre entered Windsor Castle*

When Alixandre had remounted, then if any knight ever did marvels, he
did, for of the archers there were not twenty left who had not been put to
the sword by the fine performance of Alixandre and Sir Gauvain. The count
of Windsor saw the work that these two knights were accomplishing, which
gave him such a fright that he fled by a secret path. Alixandre saw him when
he was about two arpents or measures of land away; and he told himself he
would prevent his ruse – but may God allow him to accomplish his goal!
He saw that the great throng of traitors had decreased and was now much
diminished, and he saw also that those of his party had nothing to fear, for
the king was very close by watching the battle and ready to help his men, if
need be. Alixandre called about ten of his men and had them put down their
shields and take up those of their enemies that were lying on the ground,
and even, after this, he had them take their enemies' horses. Then, when they
had donned their adversaries' arms, he withdrew into a secret path near a
thicket and said to his men, 'In order to enable us to enter Windsor Castle,
which is being guarded now by the evil count along with a few cowardly
and recreant knights, I have had you arm yourselves with the shields of
these people so that when we arrive at the gate they will believe that we
are their friends and will leave the gate open and unguarded. Once inside,
let us, with God's grace, seize and bind the disloyal man whom Fortune
considers the enemy while favoring [p. 93] us, for we have a just cause and

---

[17] 'thick': for a lacuna that occurred here, Foerster, p. 298, proposed 'en la plus <grant> presse'.
See Colombo Timelli, p. 173.

a good right to do this. Follow me,' said Alixandre, 'and, if it depends on you, we will win the day.'

Then they set out. They came to the castle gate, and those who saw them, believing that they were the same men who had issued forth shortly before, let them in peacefully, without anyone addressing them until they had passed the third bridge, the third wall, and the third iron gate, and found themselves in the main courtyard where the count and several squires and knights were standing: barely eight of them were wearing sallet, hauberk, or coat of mail.

22. *How Alixandre attacked those of the castle and killed a great many*

Alixandre, finding himself as mentioned above in the main courtyard, sought to accomplish his goal, for he saw his enemies within his grasp. First, he had the three gates closed and the bridges raised, then he had the gate keeper killed and thrown over the outer wall into the moats; and when he had done that, he shouted to his enemies: 'Death to you! Death to you!' At these words the enemy sallied forth crying, 'Betrayed, we are betrayed! You, our prince, take up your arms and think to protect your head, for you are in danger of dying.' Then Alixandre settled himself firmly in his stirrups and shouted, 'Attack, attack!' Next, he couched his lance and at the first contact pierced through one, then killed a second, and all those he struck were slain and put to death. His men did likewise and proved valiant. The count was very distressed, and upon seeing Alixandre he singled him out as the best knight. He couched his lance and came to joust against Alixandre's shield with such force that his lance split into more than six pieces. At that point, Alixandre had no lance, and when he saw that his enemy had broken his lance against his shield, he rode straight up to him and, on the attack, struck him so hard with shield, body, and might that he felled knight and horse, with both landing in a pile. On suffering this blow, the count totally lost heart. He [p. 94] no longer had his wits about him, and he saw these ten Greek knights fighting so well that, no longer knowing whose men they were and hoping to save his soul until help arrived, he fled with a great number of men into a room that was perilous to enter because the passage was narrow. Those who could not get to the door of the room in enough time begged for mercy, and Alixandre took them to the battlements and made them jump off from that height: it was every man for himself. But in order to prevent the count from fleeing, he stationed two strong and confident knights there.

23. *How Alixandre vanquished several people from the castle.*

After accomplishing these actions, Alixandre looked about until he found at least twenty armed men in a ditch who had settled there to rest as they had been up all night. He cried out, 'Death to you!' upon which they woke up and grabbed their good swords, saying they were not afraid of eight men. Angrily they came toward Alixandre, who began to strike out with such force that it seemed that his blows cost him nothing. He killed one of them and then a second one with only two blows, at which point the others, believing that he was a devil, surrendered to him. Alixandre took their swords, then made them go up to the battlements and, as he had done with the others as a reward for their rebellion and malevolence, he made them jump into the moats where they died miserably.

Then Alixandre came back to the first gate and found there many tired and recreant men-at-arms. They cried out to be let inside, and then one of the gate keepers, in order to save his life, fell on his knees before Alixandre and said that if he would pardon him, he would find a way to deliver to him the heads of all those who wished to enter. Alixandre agreed. Then the gate keeper showed himself to those outside and told them that if they wished to enter, it would have [p. 95] to be by the postern gate and, to make sure that none of the enemy was among them, they should remove their helmets and come in one by one in single file. Those outside were pleased to comply. The gate keeper lowered the plank of the postern gate, which he held closed, and with each one who came, as they entered he took them to a room where Alixandre was and cut off the heads of all of them; in that way he saved his life.

Finally, after this very great massacre of the traitors, Alixandre found in his path an enormous club and, sheathing his sword, he picked up the club and headed for the room where the count was. Outside he found a great thug who was fighting against his knights. Alixandre saw him, raised the club, and gave him such a hard blow that he knocked him over, causing him to fall on the ground in a heap. Then Alixandre put one foot into the narrow passage, and when he had cleared the path of the third, fourth, and fifth man, he saw the count hiding near a post with a large ax in his hand. Alixandre raised his club again and, after a long chase – for the count kept turning around the post – he jumped forward and struck him on the top of his helmet with such might that he stunned him and forced him, with his head spinning, back against the walls of the room, where he stopped and fell in a heap, all sense and memory gone.

24. How Alixandre stripped the count of Windsor bare on the wall and uttered several insults.

When Alixandre saw that his enemy was weary, vanquished, and bereft of force, he seized him and took him prisoner, and the other Greeks, who had already gained passage, advanced. Those inside, seeing their leader totally defeated, broke rank, and were taken, seized, and [p. 96] led to the outer wall, then thrown into the moat like the others. Thus, the count remained a prisoner, alone and abandoned, in the hands of his enemies.

I shall pass over Sir Gauvain's exploits and those of King Arthur's noble princes, who, after complete victory and on finding Alixandre's armor on a corpse, believed it was he. Thus, they mourned him with anguish, weeping copiously over the death of the very Alixandre who at this hour had climbed up to the top of the outer wall and was presenting to the entire town their count, whom he had bound with rope and stripped down to his fine shift. Whoever might wish to find a man without a single dram of joy could quite legitimately choose this treacherous count who, seeing himself defeated and in the clutches of his enemies, cursed the hour that he had been born. He despised his miserable, filthy, evil life, and, committing blasphemy, he said, 'Oh, how Fortune is against me, since she binds and subjects me to the planet that was reigning at the hour and minute that I was conceived. I believe that God, as soon as He created me from a lump of earth, allowed me to be the most evil man who ever was, is, and ever will be, and it seems that I was created with the intention that I should never in my life have anything but diabolical temptations, by which this evil, misfortune, shame, loss, and damnation have come to attend my most miserable end.' Then he turned toward Alixandre saying, 'You, who hold me bound by thick, heavy ropes, kill the unfortunate man that I am so that I may be delivered once and for all from what I might expect to endure.'

'You should not have such a good fate,' said Alixandre. 'Justice will be served in time for the great number of your criminal acts, which [p. 97] are the cause of the destruction and perdition of the great people who, because of your irrational intentions, have been executed and put to death today, following much bloodshed. Now see with what grievous affliction and suffering your flesh will surely be tormented to compensate for your crime and this great loss of the people you had seduced, bewitched, and suborned with your false words.' The townspeople, seeing their prince naked, bound, and vilely insulted, and even pointed out as an example, begged Alixandre's mercy, but he enjoined them to go tell King Arthur that Alixandre was holding the count prisoner. Hearing these words, all the townspeople went off toward the battlefield, where they saw by chance the Britons exalting and rushing toward the castle pursuing some of the count's complicit knights who truly thought they could escape.

Finally, when it was learned that Alixandre was holding the fortress and the count prisoner, the tears of the king and of everyone else turned to joy, and they took heart. They found their enemies at the bridge witnessing the count's unfortunate fate, and in this posture they were surprised and put to death. I do not say that quite a few did not escape by making a successful flight. But Alixandre, on seeing the king, had the castle gates thrown open, and when he and his men had gone inside, their banner was planted at the highest point. Alixandre delivered his prisoner to the king, who had the count beheaded and quartered and his head stuck at the end of a lance and placed in the middle of the first gate.

After this, there is no need to ask what praise was given to God for the fine performance of this very resourceful knight, Alixandre. He was given the golden cup with the consent of all. Moreover, the king asked him to request something else, saying that no gift could ever be so great that he would not grant it, except for what pertained to his own honor. Alixandre thanked him a hundred thousand times, as he was so skilled at doing, but it happened that he dared not request what he desired. [p. 98] He knew full well that if he requested it, it would not be denied, but because he was afraid that it might displease someone – that is, if the king gave him Soredamors to be his wife – he asked for a day's leave to decide, which the king granted.

25. *How the queen questioned Alixandre about his desires.*

Now that Alixandre had the golden cup, he thought he would give it to a good friend, and, because of the great esteem in which he held Sir Gauvain, he presented it to him and begged him over and over to accept it until he did, which made Alixandre very happy. The news of these events spread everywhere, and Soredamors found out. Shortly before, she had heard that her beloved was dead, giving rise to thoughts that brought on tears and weeping, but now she rejoiced so heartily that the sad thoughts and great suffering she had just experienced were driven out and put behind her. She wiped her eyes and washed her tear-stained face, telling her heart that it should rejoice. But she found Alixandre's extended absence worrisome.

Alixandre likewise was anxious to see his beautiful beloved, and for this reason, because of his great desire, as soon as he returned to his tents he proceeded on to the tents of the queen whom he met and greeted honorably. The queen, who could not celebrate Alixandre enough, returned his greeting, then took him to a splendid tent and, knowing what would be the greatest pleasure she could give him, now summoned her niece Soredamors and had him sit down next to her. Then she began to address the knight in this way: 'Now then, Alixandre, my most loyal servant, you who seek adventure and ask yourself the ways and means to arrive at an exalted state, know that your gracious behavior has made me certain that Love's powers are working in such a way that through attentive effort [p. 99] you strive to serve a certain young lady of high station by admiring her intelligence, beauty, and refinement. And because I have pity on you, I wish to know if, as your secretary and advocate in this matter, I can help you, as one who willingly and wholeheartedly agrees to assist you in this task.'

When Alixandre saw that the queen understood his situation, he blushed and, wishing to conceal his feelings no longer, told her, 'Thank you, my lady, for the offer you are making me: I am not worthy of it, but, with regard to the desires to which you have given a name, I do not wish to exclude myself; rather, I grant that your words are true and consider myself subject to the god of Love. And so, my lady, if it pleases you to know my state in this matter, I confess that my heart has truly been wounded by my love for the most gracious young lady to be found among one hundred thousand ladies of whatever beauty they may possess. So it is not without reason that my eyes hold my heart in servitude in order to acquire the good grace of this beauty, and, if I were fortunate enough that she might wish to have mercy on me, as God and my soul are witness, I would believe that I am[18] the servant who is best rewarded by Love that any knight ever was. Alas, my lady, I can no longer conceal my feelings, rather I must name for you the woman I love, that is, my most excellent, sovereign, and desirable mistress Soredamors, who is here present, whom I beg – and you as well – with all my might to attenuate my anguished suffering.'

26. How the queen told Soredamors to take Alixandre for her husband.

In saying these words, Alixandre and the young lady changed color a hundred times, and sent forth a thousand sighs toward each other's heart as ambassadors and to solicit their wishes. The queen, knowing Soredamors's situation, that she had never [p. 100] loved any other knight, wished to question her, saying, 'Oh, my beautiful young lady, since you have heard the most humble supplication of the best of the best, who is dying to obtain your good grace, which no other has ever been able to acquire, now here is this most perfect specimen of beauty who asks to have you as his wife, lady, and mistress. Consider that he is of high station and, if your natural disdain has not been conquered by Love, you will never arrive at such a good fate as is presented by this one, who above all the knights in the entire world is renowned for being courageous, valiant, and of good lineage.'

'Alas, my lady, I would consider myself fortunate if I were good enough that this knight should deign to love me. If this great good comes to me, it would be fortunate, and may it never please God that I should refuse it, for in this world I believe I could never be more reassured.'

Then the queen sent for the king, Sir Gauvain, and the barons, who came and, having heard about the situation of the two lovers, were never so joyful. The king had them betrothed and married, but our account is silent regarding the meal, dances, jousts, and entertainment. Everyone was very happy that they were in love, and the king even held a round table and gave Alixandre all the honors he could imagine and provide. And to be brief, Alixandre and Soredamors, united in a single desire, performed their marriage vows so well multiple times that after nine months Soredamors was delivered of a very handsome son, who was named Cligés and about whom we will compose the present story.

---

[18] 'am': Foerster, p. 302, proposed 'estre' for this lacuna ('je cuideroie <estre> le serviteur ...'). See also Colombo Timelli, p. 174, who notes that it could also be rendered: 'je <me> cuideroie le serviteur'.

27. How Alix had himself crowned emperor
on the report of a liar

While Cligés was nursing and Alixandre was at King Arthur's court, the emperor and queen of Constantinople died at the same time and, when the emperor's funeral was over, the nobles, knowing that [p. 101] Alixandre was the heir, sent messengers summoning him to come take possession of the empire. The messengers set out by sea, but by misfortune all perished except one, who returned to the palace of Constantinople and told the nobles that Alixandre and all his men had perished at sea in a seasonal storm, and that of all those who had been with him he was the only one to escape. With this news, everyone made great mourning throughout the city, but in the end Alix crowned himself and took the pledge of homage and fealty from his men. But the story recounts that Alixandre soon after heard the news of his father's death. So he took leave of the king, the queen, and Sir Gauvain, and told them that his father the emperor had died and said that he would go take possession of the empire, which made the king very happy. He handed over to him ships, men, food, gold and silver, and with a great profusion of tears Alixandre put to sea, taking with him his wife and his dear son Cligés.

But here our tale will cease to speak of King Arthur and his company, and, to complete the account of Alixandre's exploits, it will state that after setting off, he found himself in the port of Constantinople and discovered that his brother Alix was wearing the imperial crown.

28. How an accommodation was made between
Alix and Alixandre

When Alixandre learned that his brother had appropriated and granted to himself a right that did not belong to him, he was not pleased, and he ordered him to return the realm to him or he would seek a remedy. Alix, knowing that Alixandre was alive, did not know what to say, and he was very sick at heart. He summoned the council, and after deliberation was obliged to humble himself before his brother. An accommodation was made between him and Alixandre according to which Alix would only wear the crown and never take a wife, and Alixandre, for his part, would have all the benefits and would be honored as emperor [p. 102] in exchange for a certain sum of deniers that he would deliver to his brother Alix every year of his life. In this way, Alix and Alixandre reigned for a long time.

But it happened finally that Alixandre and Soredamors fell ill. Soredamors died, and Alixandre, feeling gravely ill, summoned his child Cligés, who was already grown and had reached adulthood, and said to him: 'Cligés, my son, my heart's joy, be certain that you will never obtain honor if you do not go to serve King Arthur. Therefore, if Adventure takes you there, I beg you to behave wisely and to make the acquaintance of your uncle, Sir Gauvain, for among all the others, he has the greatest renown and is the one who for love of me will willingly promote you.' He had scarcely finished speaking when his soul left his body, which caused great grief for Cligés and Alix, who had him solemnly buried. And thus ended the life of Alixandre, Cligés's father, about whom we have made a brief account,[19] and now we shall begin the second account as follows.[20]

29. *Here follows the second part of this story, which*
contains this chapter about how Alix's counselors
advised him to take a wife

For a long time following the death of Alixandre and Soredamors, Alix kept his promise never to take a wife. But since there is nothing that time does not make us forget, some of Alix's advisors, who were young and unreasonable, so exhorted him to marry that he forgot his oath and was pleased to take a wife, provided that she was extraordinarily beautiful. The advisors answered that such a thing would not be [p. 103] difficult; for, in response to an inquiry they had made, they were aware that the emperor of Germany had a daughter who was the most beautiful of a hundred thousand ladies. They told Alix what they knew about the beautiful maiden, and he, already enamored of her, quickly sent his ambassadors to the emperor to solicit the beautiful lady in his name.

Having departed and set out, they found themselves in the city of Ratisbon, where the emperor was then staying. They went to him and, in short, after paying their respects to the emperor, asked him for his daughter Fenice to be given in marriage to the emperor of Constantinople. The German emperor said he would willingly speak to his daughter and his council and, when he had heard from both that nothing but good could come of this alliance, he granted his daughter to the ambassadors for and in the name of the emperor of Constantinople. They were very joyful and thanked the emperor profusely, and he gave them a warm welcome and, after great mutual rejoicing expressed in words, gestures, and food, as well as in dances, gifts, and entertainment, the emperor called them together and said to them, 'Now then, fair lords and friends, since it has been arranged that I have given you my daughter to have an equal share in and be the lady of the empire of Constantinople, for which she will have to be taken from my house to Greece, I am most joyful. But it happens that the duke of Saxony has already asked me for her several times and wants to make her his wife. So if he learned of this and wanted to stop

---

[19] The redactor uses the term 'traitié' (= treatise).
[20] Between the end of this chapter and the beginning of the next, the scribe left a blank space equivalent to eight lines, presumably intended for the illuminator.

her, you would not be able to take her unless you had a lot of men to defend her against him. For this reason, you will have to return to your lord the emperor and, when you have greeted him for me, you will tell him that if he wants to have my child he will have to come in person, for the above-stated reason.'

[p.104] 30. *How the emperor of Constantinople went to Germany to wed Fenice*

When the Greeks had heard the emperor's message, they promised to deliver it. They took leave of him and Fenice and then set out and, thanks to their best efforts, soon found themselves back in Constantinople standing before their lord, to whom they delivered the recommendations and recounted their exploit. And because he had to go in person, Alix had robes made for his entourage and ordered his horses to be equipped with new harnesses entirely covered in gold work, pearls, and splendid disks of gilded silver. After these things had been done and his people assembled, he set out in great pomp and went his way until he arrived in the city of Cologne, where the emperor of Germany had gone to hold his court at a great feast that was in progress. Upon learning of the arrival of the emperor of Constantinople, the emperor of Germany went to greet him with a noble company of barons and, when they had arrived before the palace and Alix had dismounted, the German emperor took him by the arm and led him to his hall. Then was Fenice brought before her father, radiant with such exquisite beauty that no matter how much one said about her feminine virtues, it would not do her justice. And because I would be incapable of describing the face and very exquisite form of this beautiful young lady, I shall refrain from doing so and say that everyone marveled upon seeing her.

31. *How Fenice and Cligés first gazed upon each other*

The maiden's name suited her perfectly: it was Fenice, and just as the phoenix has a plumage unlike any other, it was the same for the young lady. For she was the best of the best, peerless, and no other woman [p. 105] was worthy of being compared to a third of her lofty beauty. And, truly, everyone said that it was impossible for Nature, despite her cleverness, to be able to compose out of nothing a masterpiece like this one.

And to return to our story, Fenice entered the palace with her head un-covered such that everyone could see her well-proportioned face. As she made her way, she saw Cligés on whom she gazed willingly, for all his limbs were well formed, and moreover he was in the flower of the age when one becomes enamored, that is, between seventeen and eighteen years of age. But Narcissus, who fell in love with his reflection in the fountain, was not more handsome than this Cligés, who was so comely that all Nature's beautiful gifts seemed amassed in him and, as gold exceeds the color of copper, by that much and more Cligés surpassed the beautiful forms of other men, like one born from a beautiful flower. His hair was like his mother's, his face was as fresh as the rose in May, and moreover he was so well fashioned as to nose, mouth, eyes, eyebrows, forehead, torso, arms, and legs that Nature, if she were to work on a million men, would not be able to make another such form, unless she asked permission from God, for whom nothing is impossible.

When Fenice has come before her father, she immediately makes a great curtsy as if he were God. Then she is seated next to her father the emperor. Cligés, who sees her thus honored, cannot look away without Love diverting and turning his eyes toward her. And she does likewise toward Cligés, who is of such fine bearing that she becomes enamored of him – not without cause, but rightly so, for he is legitimately the emperor of Constantinople to whom she has been given, and it seems to me that God does not want her to be deceived. In any case, He, who can do as He wishes, will see to it. [p. 106] The more Fenice observes Cligés's confident bearing the more she loves him. She grants him her heart as Cligés grants her his, saying to herself, 'To what great felicity God would raise me if I have arrived here at such a propitious moment that I could obtain the love of the one who surpasses in every way the most perfect men on earth.' Cligés speaks to himself in a similar vein, so that I can say that Love causes their two thoughts to come together in a single and fixed desire, and it seems to me that they are struck by Love's arrows equally and in the same measure. Imbued with a perfect desire and a single thought, Cligés and Fenice turn their eyes and attention to admiring the sweetness, beauty, and lofty work of which each is the perfect bodily form.

But now our account will leave them gazing upon each other and proceed to speak of the actions of the duke of Saxony, who was so enamored of Fenice that, although he had been refused several times, he had sent his nephew and at least five hundred men with him to go speak to the emperor yet again about the marriage of his daughter.

32. *How Archadés defied the emperors, and Cligés responded*

In this part, the story tells that the duke of Saxony's nephew reached Cologne on the very day that the emperor of Constantinople had arrived, and to execute his mission, he found himself at the palace standing before the emperor, saying, 'Sire, God save you and increase your honor if you would condescend to accept the supplication that the duke of Saxony is making to you. Since it is the case that he has several times asked for your daughter in marriage, wishing to increase her honor and wealth, and you have refused to comply, this time he wishes to know if you will do so or not. And should you deign to give her to me, he will love you, and, [p. 107] if not, he will wage war against you and your people.'

To these words neither the emperor nor any knight or anyone else responded, acting so out of disdain. Seeing this, the duke of Saxony's nephew challenged them. No one reacted to this challenge, but because Cligés wished to demonstrate his power, he addressed this Saxon named Archadés, saying, 'You, knight, who are so bold as to challenge my uncle the emperor, and from whom you claim arrogantly what has been granted to him, leave this place and take three hundred of your companions, and I shall meet you with two hundred of mine. And I shall prove on this day by the sword and lance which of us has the better right – you to attack me or me to defend myself.'

At these words, Archadés left to do what Cligés had charged him to do. Cligés was promptly surrounded by knights owing to the bravery they saw in him. He took two hundred of the least experienced and, before they were fitted out in their armor on one side and the other, the emperor and his beautiful daughter, with ladies and maidens, went up to the battlements overlooking the field on which the knights of both sides would come together.[21]

33. *How the Greeks and Saxons fought against each other*

When Cligés and Archadés were ready, seeing that it was time to get to work, they spurred their horses toward each other, and God knows if they spared lances or shields. On one side Cligés acquitted himself well, and on the other the Saxon knight did a very good job of piercing shields, breaking lances, and striking great blows on these helmets and hauberks. Cligés saw this and turned in that direction, riding like [p. 108] the wind and slashing everything before him, and there where he saw Archadés fighting haughtily, he rode up to him and struck such a blow with his lance that he unsaddled him and sent him sprawling onto the grass of the field. Then Cligés charged into the thick of the fray and, before his lance could fail, he fought so well with it that no other knight could have done better than he. Nevertheless, he broke his lance against a knight armed like a Turk in boiled leather, then he seized his sword and sent flying so many heads, arms, and hands that all those who saw him fighting marveled how a single man had the force that Cligés had to fell so many men and cause so many horses to tumble and fall. For he did not attach more importance to killing the best Saxon knights, nor did it trouble him to provoke another to strike a blow. This is why his strengths outshone the exploits of all the others in this battle as gold outshines the six types of metals.

34. *How Cligés fought marvelously in the battle or joust*

While Cligés was performing so well, the Saxons had great difficulty getting Archadés remounted, which they were not able to do without causing the death of forty knights or squires. For he was struck back down five

---

[21] Between the end of this chapter and the beginning of the next, the scribe left a blank space equivalent to nine lines, presumably intended for the illuminator.

times before he could remount, and after this scrimmage, he gathered up his strength and did so much with the good help of his men that he got himself remounted on a very good steed. Then Archadés became puffed up with pride and swore disdainfully that he would avenge his shame. He thrust himself into the thick of the fray and, as best he could, wreaked vengeance against the Greeks, who confronted him with such skill that they could no longer have dishonor that day. For even though the Greeks were only two against three, Cligés encouraged them and made them resist and drive against their enemies so relentlessly that the Saxons [p. 109] could not find a way to make them retreat a single time.

Archadés was enraged when he found that the Greeks were so sure of themselves in combat. He ran all about and sought out Cligés so diligently among the ranks that he found him and saw him removing the arms from Archadés's men – swords from their hands, shields from their necks, and helmets from their heads. This sight encouraged him more than before, so he attacked him and dealt him such a sword blow to his shield that he broke off a whole half of one of its quarters. Cligés was scarcely pleased. Recognizing his enemy by his arms, he greeted him with such a high, hard sword blow to his helmet that he stunned him and felled him a second time. Seeing this, the Saxons did not know what to do but finally with all their might they helped Archadés remount. Archadés took heart and rallied and reassembled his men with the sound of his horn. And for a third time he thrust himself into the battle to the misfortune of those who followed him, for the farther they went the more they were struck down by the blows that Cligés dealt them. Their great number decreased and diminished. They no longer were brave enough to defend themselves; rather, they were forced to beat a vile retreat because of the prowess of this single squire, Cligés, aided by his men.

The beautiful young lady, Fenice, was on the battlements and willingly watched Cligés and told herself that here was a valiant champion. The Saxons turned their backs, increasing the boldness of the Greeks, who had the advantage and pursued and accompanied them as far as a little river they had to cross. Cligés rushed in that direction and forced so many of them to bathe in the river that there were more than one hundred who saved themselves in this way, for Cligés did not deign to pursue them farther, telling himself that he would obtain little honor by killing these faint hearts, since they did not have the power to defend themselves, and he saw them tossing their swords into the distance.

[p.110] 35. *How Thessala questioned Fenice*
about the cause of her sorrow

As mentioned above, Cligés allowed the Saxons to pull each other out of the river where he had driven them. He headed back hale and hearty and, when he passed before the Greeks and Germans, beautiful Fenice repaid him with a sweet and amorous look for his fine performance, and Cligés responded likewise by Love's encouragement. When everyone had returned to the palace, all the talk was of Cligés's deeds. And the ladies and maidens asked the Greeks who was this noble young man Cligés who had done so well. It was thus that Fenice learned that he was to be emperor of Constantinople if he received his right, and that his uncle Alix, who was then wearing the crown of the empire, was going back on his oath by wanting to take her for his wife, for since he possessed the crown unjustly, he had promised Alixandre never to marry. God, how seized Fenice was with love for Cligés! 'Alas,' she said, 'I was born in an evil hour if this false and faithless perjurer obtains what he claims! Certainly,[22] I am determined and resolved in my decision to love Cligés, to whom I have been given, since he should by right have the jurisdiction and empire of Constantinople.'

Then she considered how she would be able to realize this project and, when she had reflected at length and not found a way, never was a maiden more sorrowful. Thessala, her nurse,[23] looked at her and, although she was instructed in the science of necromancy and very expert in enchantments, she could not discover on her own the cause of Fenice's sorrow. So she turned to her and began speaking thus, 'My child, I am amazed to see your sweet face, for it is alternately white and vermilion, and it seems from an examination of your bearing that you are plunged in sorrow. And for this reason, I beg to know your trouble, and I have no doubt that I can cure your malady. [p. 111] For never did Medea or anyone else know the tricks that I can do with medicine, and indeed with the invisible, magical, and enchanting science of which you have not heard me speak. And, by the faith that I owe you, there is nothing I would not do to relieve you and preserve your honor.'

36. How Thessala inquired of Fenice about the cause of her malady

Fenice, though hearing Thessala speak so graciously, still did not dare reveal her thinking, lest she be dissuaded from wanting to love Cligés; and she feared also that Thessala might discover it by magic. And yet, she accepted her nurse's oath that she would keep the secret and would not reveal to anyone – for loss or gain or for good or evil – anything Fenice might tell her. And when Thessala swore to her that she would be secretive and reliable, Fenice began to speak, 'To you, my nurse, who are questioning me,

---

[22] There follows in Colombo Timelli's edition 'quelque chose <...>' but neither she nor Foerster proposed anything to fill this lacuna.

[23] In the prose as in the verse *Cligés*, Thessala is referred to both by the narrator and the heroine as Fenice's 'mestresse'. We have followed the practice of most translators by rendering the term as 'nurse' or 'governess', but it actually indicates the great respect that Thessala has earned for her skill as an empiric, someone who has not been formally trained in medicine. See Laine E. Doggett, *Love Cures. Healing and Love Magic in Old French Romance*. Penn State Romance Studies (University Park, PA, 2009), ch. 2.

your child, regarding the cause of my sorrow, I declare to you, on condition of loyalty, that the sorrow I feel seems to me both sweet and painful, and I would not want for anything in the world not to have this malady, which has befallen me in such a way that, if I wanted to cure or rid myself of it, my heart would not be content. For it tells me that the malady I am suffering cannot hurt me, as bitter as it is, as I now suffer pain and misery from it, and also joy and happiness at the same time.'

On hearing these words Thessala knew full well that Fenice did not have what she desired in love, and she answered, 'Oh, child, I perceive that there is nothing more certain than that Love holds you in his thrall so closely that the pains your body bears through Hope seem to you at the same time to be made of soothing [p. 112] and honey-sweet oils, for it is the nature of Love's malady that it seems at one point the most pleasurable experience ever and at the next the most grievous one that a person can suffer or bear. So I must understand that your pain is caused by an effect of Love. And in any case, if you love, I do not wish to say that this is a bad thing, for a lady without love will never obtain joy or pleasure; rather, she will be hard, sad, clumsy, and endowed with a rude, unsubtle understanding, and so neglected, that no one will take any account of her. Confess your case to me, my lady, and, if it is possible that any woman can help you, I will do so much that you will be happy.'

'Nurse,' said Fenice, 'since it is the case that I trust you, I can tell you that I am most unhappy that my father is giving me as wife to the false perjuring old man of Constantinople, whom I could neither cherish nor love. For my love is settled, by an extraordinary event, on the most handsome man who lives under heaven, namely, Cligés. And I do not know what I can do, for I would rather be dismembered than have my body abused and debased by two men as was that of Yseult, Tristan's beloved, which was always delivered over to two – in fact, the body was, but not the heart – , for such a love would not be right. And, so help me God, he who will have my heart, he alone will be master of my body. But woe is me, I do not know how I can give my body to the one on whom my heart is set, for I dare not gainsay my father, who has betrothed me to a man other than my beloved. And he, being a man of his word, will necessarily want to keep his promise, and I do not know what I should do about it, and I beg you, Nurse, to kindly advise me. And so that you do not believe that I am embracing an evil cause and doing wrong, I shall have you know that Cligés is the son of the late Alixandre, [p. 113] elder brother of Alix, who wrongly rules the empire, which belongs to Cligés. And you know that I am given in marriage to the rightful emperor, which is why I wish, come what may, that the gift be realized, for Cligés, though he be deprived of his right, should have a beautiful maiden of high station, and I hope that God will help him.'

Fenice had barely finished her speech when Thessala promised her that she would contrive by means of potions and incantations that the wicked emperor would never touch her when she was in bed with him, no more than if there were a wall between the two of them. She would do this by means of a beverage that she would have Alix taste, one that would have the power to ensure that he would never be able to kiss or embrace a woman except in his sleep, for then he would think he was awake and having great pleasure with her.

37. How Fenice was wed, and Thessala prepared the drink

This response comforted Fenice and gave her great hope, and she swore to her eyes and her heart that she would not fail to keep her promise to them and that she would have none other than Cligés, for he seemed very worthy of having a beautiful lady. And, in short, night passed, and the next day was the perfect wedding of Fenice and Alix, which filled the palace with joy.

And while the ladies dance and the knights and squires are engaged in jousts and tournaments, we shall speak of Thessala, Fenice's nurse, who, as she had promised, prepared her magic potion full of sweet spices to make it more delicious to drink.

38. How Cligés served his uncle the magic potion

At the appropriate moment, Thessala had perfected her magic and, when she saw the emperors seated at the table and had tried to think of someone who could accomplish her goal, she decided there was no man [p. 114] more worthy or suitable for this task than Cligés, who was serving his uncle at table: he was the one toward whom the messengers should make their way. In the end, Thessala winked at Cligés, who went to speak to her. She instructed him very carefully and gave him the potion to put in Alix's golden cup, serving it only to him and saying that it was intended for newly weds, and he was to make sure not to give it to anyone except his uncle. But first, so that Cligés would not hesitate to do this, Thessala took a sip, knowing full well how to guard against the power of the drink. Cligés then served the magic wine to his uncle. It seemed good to Alix, and he drank it very willingly, for it permeated his whole body, and it seemed to him that his heart opened because of the drink that had its effect within him.

39. How Alix dreamed that he was kissing and caressing Fenice

After supper and the dances and entertainment were over, and the bed blessed, Fenice was undressed and taken to her chamber, then put to bed toward one side. Soon after, Alix went to bed, but he was not lying totally inside the sheets when he fell asleep, and by the power of the potion he began to dream, believing that he was holding his beloved in his arms. It seemed to him that he kissed her a hundred thousand times and that he caressed her breasts, but she resisted; and it seemed to him that she did not want to kiss or embrace him, just like other virgins on the first night that they sleep with their husbands; but it seemed to him that she finally surrendered, as much by love as by force; and it seemed to him that he had never had greater delectation than he had with her; then it seemed to him that he let her go, and after turning his back to her fell asleep. And when he awoke finally, he got up very happy and found his beautiful maiden dressed and ready, and from then on she did not go to bed until her husband was asleep and always got up before he was awake. And in [p. 115] such reveries he was and would be engaged without ever having a single kiss from her, for he did not attach any importance to it during the day, since he believed he would have his fill while dreaming.

We shall now suspend for a time our account of the relations between Fenice and Alix and proceed to speak of the duke of Saxony.

40. How Archadés recounted his misfortune to his uncle, the duke

The story tells that Archadés, after his defeat, returned sorrowful and sad to Saxony and told his uncle, the duke, that he should have no more expectations regarding Fenice, for she had been promised and granted to the emperor of Constantinople, 'who is very powerful and has in his company a nephew who is most valiant, and in fact when we met in pitched battle he killed several of my knights and manhandled us to such an extent that he did as he wished and pleased with me.'

Oh, how sad and sorrowful was the duke! He was out of his mind and swore he would die if he did not take vengeance on the Greeks. He assembled his entire force and sent his knights by several paths to form an ambush and block the passage, and he even charged spies to go daily to Cologne for news and to tell him all that was being done and organized at the court of the emperors. Alix, after participating in a great, joyful, and solemn celebration both on his wedding day and for several days afterwards, wanted to depart and return to Greece. He set out with a very great company, including the German emperor and his barons, taking his wife Fenice whom he loved dearly, although she did not love him but rather cherished the man who for love of her did not have a single hour of repose.[24]

[p. 116] 41. How Cligés killed Archadés, the duke of Saxony's nephew

The Germans and Greeks made such good time that they crossed the Danube River at around the fifth hour of the evening and made their encampment in

---

[24] Between the end of this chapter and the beginning of the next, the scribe left a blank space equivalent to nine lines, presumably intended for the illuminator.

a meadow where they set up their pavilions and made so much noise that the duke of Saxony, who was guarding this passage with a large army in a forest located near that plain, heard them. He sent his nephew Archadés to go and find out who these people were. Archadés armed himself and set out with five others, and when he came to the edge of the forest, he saw Cligés, who, engaged in thoughts of his beloved, was leading his horse about along with two of his squires. Archadés saw him within his reach and, recognizing him, told himself he would take vengeance on him, and thus he set out and dismounted so stealthily alongside a larch that Cligés did not see him until he was about to strike. The Saxon knight advanced, then, and Cligés, turning around, was struck on his shield, which broke into pieces under the iron of the lance. Then, Cligés, ready to joust, attacked his enemy with such violence that he pierced him through and through and tossed his corpse to the other Saxons, who, trembling with fear, took flight. Cligés, unaware of the ambush, pursued them and in fact killed two of them.

Meanwhile, the others had enough time to return to the duke who, on hearing of the death of his nephew Archadés, summoned Thierry, one of his knights, to whom he promised a great reward if he could once and for all bring him Cligés's head. Thierry said that he would not delay in doing so if the knight should dare to wait for him. Then, confident of his strength – for he was tall, young, and arrogant, and indeed [p. 117] was considered to be the duke's club – after hearing how he could recognize Cligés, he set out and found Cligés in the valley where he had killed Archadés. At that point he was all alone, for his squires had fled in order to relate to the emperors what he had done.

Thierry approached Cligés and, as soon as he could, shouted at him like a foolish and arrogant man, saying, 'Oh, wicked man, you who just killed my lord Archadés, flee from here if you can, for, since I can strike you, I know well that you will die from it, for I will now cut off your head and present it to my lord the duke, who wants nothing else as recompense for the death you inflicted on his most beloved nephew.'

'Vassal,' said Cligés, 'when by your hand you have slain the servant who for the sake of Love undertakes the exercise of arms, then will you be in a position to do what you please with his head, but first you will have to prevail while wielding lance or sword, and, if I can, I shall prevent you from doing so.'

Then they spurred their good horses and positioned their shields, settled themselves firmly in their stirrups, lowered their lances,[25] and clashed with all their might. Thierry broke his lance, and Cligés with his dealt such a good, strong blow to his enemy's chest that he pierced him through clear to the heart and made him tumble onto the grass. Next, Cligés dismounted and unlaced the knight's helmet, then cut off his head and stuck it on the end of his lance. Moreover, he took his horse, helmet, and shield, and, equipping himself with

[25] The word 'lances' is suggested by both Foerster, p. 312, and Colombo Timelli, pp. 117 and 179, to fill a lacuna.

them, set off, such that the knights of Greece and Constantinople who saw him were greatly distressed, for on seeing him at a distance they thought it was Cligés's head. So they ran after him, and Cligés, who wished to see the [p. 118] battle between the duke and his uncle, continued along the main path until he arrived before the duke's army. The duke saw him and, really thinking it was Thierry, pointed him out to his men and derived great joy from it.

Cligés then sees the Greeks lined up as if to attack him and the Saxons on the other side who, seeing their enemies, ready themselves. Cligés is between the two armies. Without saying a word, he wants to make himself known, and as soon as he sees the duke of Saxony, he rushes toward him with lowered lance; and with the head still on it he goes forward to strike and confront him in such a way that if the iron had been free, it would have wounded him badly. Thereupon, Cligés shouts to the duke, 'You, who wished to have my head, take and accept this blow with that of your servant, for you certainly deserve it: one does not catch such birds with a net.'[26] Then the knights of Constantinople, having heard and seen Cligés, advance, and the Saxons, seeing that they have to defend themselves, go ahead; and at the encounter there is such a great thumping of lances against shields that for many death ensues, and a large number stumble to the ground as countless straps, bridles, reins, and breastplates rupture.

The duke saw Cligés fighting marvelously with the knight's head still at the end of his lance. He felt greatly humiliated and rushed at him so violently that each broke his lance against the other's shield, then they clashed with all their might so rudely that the duke was lifted up and straightaway sent to land on his head on the field. Then Cligés jumped on his steed, which was completely white and the best to be seen among all the good horses of Arabia. Once Cligés was mounted on it, he drew his good sword and rushed into the thick of the fray, making the ranks tremble before him.

And now we shall leave off for a while speaking of this battle, which is very fierce and bold, and proceed [p. 119] to tell briefly about something that happened during this combat to the maiden Fenice, who had remained alone with the ladies and maidens.

42. *How Fenice was carried off and entrusted to the guard of twelve knights*

Since the duke, who knew all manner of fraud and treachery, saw the Greeks far from their tents and pavilions, he, who had just been felled, thought, while catching his breath, to send a hundred knights to go seize Fenice and take her by love or force. The knights, having set out to accomplish their lord's ruse and having arrived at the tents, headed to where Fenice was and killed all the squires, boys, and men-at-arms who were there. Then they

---

[26] Cf. the proverb: 'vieil oiseau ne se prend a retz' (= one does not catch an old bird with a net). See Colombo Timelli, p. 179.

seized Fenice against her will and carried her into the woods along deserted paths to a place to which they had repaired before. Once Fenice had been taken there, just as you have heard, she was handed over to be guarded by twelve knights, and the others set out again, telling the guards that they should not move from that place until they heard the sound of the duke's horn. The duke was in the battle performing very well for the hope he had of sleeping with the maiden that night. But God will be able to prevent it. When the Saxon knights had returned to the place of battle and recounted their exploit to the duke, he rejoiced greatly.

At that point the sun slipped out of sight, and both sides sounded the retreat, saying they would come back to fight each other the next day, and they all returned to their pavilions except for Cligés, who remained behind in the hope of encountering some good escapade.

[p. 120] 43. *How the duke of Saxony sounded his horn, and six of the knights who had Fenice in custody greeted Cligés*

When the duke of Saxony learned that his enemies could well have left the forest, he sounded his horn so loudly that those who were guarding Fenice heard it. They set out, and Cligés soon saw them coming through a clearing, and he stopped. The knights saw him and, because he was mounted on their duke's steed, they thought it was their lord, so six of them came before him and greeted him loudly saying, 'Duke of Saxony, may God protect you and grant you your heart's desire. Be comforted, as you have good reason to be joyful, for the day and hour have come when we will place in your power and possession that most beautiful lady whom you have loved since the beginning of your adolescence.'[27]

44. *How Cligés killed eleven knights on a moor and recovered Fenice*

God, what great anguish and tribulation Cligés felt in his heart when he heard from the knights that they had carried off the maiden! He thought he would go out of his mind, and his heart filled with such anger and rage that never was a leopard, tiger, or lion more keen on defending its young than Cligés was determined to defend the maiden, his lady. He wanted to risk his life and never would he wish to live if he did not rescue her. So, without saying a word, he spurred on his Arabian steed and unhorsed the first knight he met; he did likewise with the second, third, fourth, fifth, and sixth, and returned their greetings in such a way that without saying much he killed them all one after the other and proved his prowess so greatly that

---

[27] Between the end of this chapter and the beginning of the next, the scribe left a blank space equivalent to about ten lines, presumably intended for the illuminator.

he seemed to have the strength of Samson, for they did not stop him any more than would six lambs in the face of a hungry she-wolf.

When he had rid the place of the first six, he realized he had done nothing if he did not deal with the [p. 121] others. Once again and even more so, he tested his good steed, which immediately jumped into action and ran so rapidly after those who held Fenice that he caught up with them and without stopping to haggle with them attacked them more violently than he had the others. And he, who wanted to fight still better, in one attack struck the first and the second with a spear in such a manner that he unhorsed them both. On seeing this, the other four were very upset, and they all advanced on Cligés to strike him with a blow of their lances, without making him retreat a single step. With their lances shattered, Cligés unsheathed his burnished sword and went to meet these four knights. With great boldness he sent the head of one knight flying to one side and his body to the other, putting the knight's companions to flight. But of the three all were slain save one, who escaped with some difficulty and, on arriving before the duke, recounted what had befallen him. On hearing about it the duke was most distressed.

When Cligés saw himself delivered of his enemies, he unlaced his helmet and approached Fenice, from whom he gently took a kiss. Oh, how joyful was Fenice when she saw her beloved Cligés kissing her. She heaved a great sigh and thanked her sweetheart a hundred thousand times, as one who henceforth would have willingly granted him her love if he had requested it. But Cligés barely dared speak to her, so much did he fear angering her with his words, which he would not have done if he had revealed his loyal thoughts; rather, it would have made her happy and put an end to her great pain.

Without speaking of what pertained to their love, Cligés brought tear-stained Fenice back safe and sound to the pavilions of the emperors, who had returned shortly before and had heard that Fenice had been carried off by a hundred knights, and the greatest joy they could muster was to make moan and lament, believing that Fenice was lost. In spite of this mourning, the emperors nevertheless dried their [p. 122] eyes when they saw Cligés bringing Fenice back with him They went forth to meet them and, when he had recounted his exploit, never had they been more joyful, and they praised God, cried 'Noël!'[28] throughout the army, and praised the noble vassal Cligés who had performed so well.

45. *How Cligés was challenged to a joust*
by the duke of Saxony

Now our account falls silent regarding the ovations that Cligés received and speaks of the duke of Saxony who, upon hearing of the death of his eleven knights and Fenice's rescue, thought suddenly that he would go out of his

---

[28] Noël!: a general exclamation of rejoicing.

mind and lay more than half an hour without getting up from where he
had fallen; indeed, all night he did not stop pulling on his hair and beard,
cursing his life, and behaving like a crazy man. As long as the night lasted,
the duke had no repose, like a man who was troubled in his heart, thoughts,
and innermost feelings. And, in short, the morning after he sent a messenger
to the emperor's tents and, having ascertained that Cligés had done him this
insolence, he challenged him to appear personally before him for a joust to
the death regarding the complaint he had against Cligés, who in his view
had wrongly kidnapped the maiden.

When the emperors heard the news, they were very distressed and answered that Cligés would not carry out the duke's bidding, but Cligés absolutely refused to accept these words. He fell at his uncle's feet, begging him
to agree to let him fight. Once Cligés's great desire and humble plea had
been considered, he was made a knight and obtained permission from the
emperor to do as he wished. He went to the herald and said the following
words: 'You who came to challenge me to a joust by order of [p. 123] your
lord, the duke of Saxony, go tell him that I, knight servant of the ladies, will
comply before an hour has elapsed on condition that he come halfway and
that his Saxons and my men arrive completely unarmed to watch us accomplish our task, leaving each of us to meet the other as the best he can.'[29]

46. How the duke of Saxony and Cligés were attacking
each other on the jousting ground

In this way the combat was sworn on both sides and, when Cligés and the
duke were ready in the same spot, they agreed on the assigned place, and
beautiful Fenice was brought out to witness the fate of the two champions,
and especially that of Cligés, for she had decided and determined that if her
beloved did not come out of this enterprise to his advantage, she would kill
herself if she did not die of rage.

When the two knights see that they are ready to begin their combat,
each one seizes his lance, and they spur their steeds so hard that it seems
as though everything will split before them; thus, they attack each other
with such force that their lances break and the duke is unhorsed, and Cligés
falls on the other side, because his steed's saddle straps break. But although
they are down, they get back on their feet expertly and have soon seized
their good swords whose blades they use to strike each other in such a way
that they make sparks of fire on their helmets and hauberks, and it seems
as though they must kill each other with each blow. Now they feel several
strong and weighty blows; each tries to save his life, and [p. 124] Cligés, who
is acquitting himself very well, gives his enemy such a blow that he makes
him bow his head and retreat a little. The duke, who out of pride grinds

---

[29] Between the end of this chapter and the beginning of the next, the scribe left a blank space
equivalent to about nine lines, presumably intended for the illuminator.

his teeth then thinks he will burst from his great ire, raises his sword and deals Cligés such a stunning blow on his helmet that he necessarily causes one of his knees to touch the ground. The Greeks are very upset, and even Fenice, who sees him struck, is overwhelmed with such grief that she cries out, 'God help him!' and says no more before falling to the ground in a faint. But you must know that she was soon raised to her feet again.

Cligés has heard this sweet word that proceeded from Fenice's sorrowful tongue. He gains in heart and spirit because he knows then that Fenice loves him in some way and, although his knee has touched the ground, he quickly raises it up and infuses it with new strength and, like one who hopes one day to have a reward for his service and who pursues only renown and honor, he summons all his strength and, for every blow with the sword point or blade that he returned previously, he now gives two; and he strives and works so hard to avenge himself that the duke is astonished at his performance and does not know what to think. For he sees this knight fiercer and more refreshed than he was at the beginning, whereas he himself feels tired and weakened from receiving the great blows that Cligés deals him. And the nicest solution he can think of is to negotiate peace in this covert manner:

'My fair young man,' said the duke to Cligés, 'I pity you since I must kill you, and this would be a shame considering the great prowess that you could acquire if you lived to maturity. And because I am already an old man, I am ashamed and hesitate to deal these overly great blows; so if you, considering my strength, beg me for mercy, perhaps I will take pity on you and pardon you for the harsh offenses and great troubles [p. 125] you have caused me.'

'Although I am still quite young,' said Cligés, 'and am made of weak cloth, compared to you, indeed, and you have dealt me great blows for a long time, in order to keep you from believing that I fear your power, I tell you that the time will never come when I will put myself at your mercy, but rather I will see our combat to its conclusion maintaining my complaint that you unjustly challenged and attacked me, and if I must I will show you that, though I am a mere child, I have the heart of a man, whatever loss there may be.'

When the duke realized that Cligés was prepared to complete his undertaking, he, who preferred to live in dishonor than to die with honor, laid down his sword, and, fearful, fell at Cligés's feet in front of everyone, saying, 'Sir knight, I surrender to you, recognizing that I have greatly offended and wronged your great nobility. I ask mercy of you, begging you to have pity on me in consideration of your nobility and chivalry, and I shall be your servant all my life.'

Then Cligés, moved to pity, raised him up and gave him leave to depart, then with great honor he returned to the Greeks, who bowed to him; and the Saxon returned like a coward to his followers, who were very happy that the war had ended by such a good means.

47[30]

That very day, the German emperor entrusted his daughter to the Greek emperor and left to return to his country. Meanwhile, Cligés, seeing that his uncle's path to Greece could not be hindered by war, decided that he wanted to go to Great Britain to carry out his father's request, [p. 126] and, as soon as he had obtained leave of the emperor, went to see Fenice and, with his head bowed toward the ground and his face covered in tears, paid his respects to her. Fenice was very distressed at seeing him weep, and Cligés went forward to make his request and beg her to give him leave to go to King Arthur's court, 'for', he said, 'I wish to apply myself to the noble exercise of arms. And because you are my sovereign lady and I have surrendered my heart and body to your service, I do not wish to go without your consent.' Fenice did not forget these sweet words, and, however much his departure grieved her, she told him she was happy to have him do as he pleased, but she could not keep from weeping. Cligés departed from her then, and, since his squires were ready, he left with many tears, accompanied by three pages mounted on three different kinds of steeds.

Our story will omit speaking of the days that Cligés spent on his trip, and will speak instead of beautiful Fenice, who remained with Alix, immersed in melancholy. For uppermost in her heart were the gracious words with which Cligés had served her upon taking leave, namely, that he had called her his sovereign lady and mistress[31] of his body and heart. 'Oh,' she said, 'what sweet words! I am not deceived, for by his bearing, and in his acts and words, he has shown me that he is my loyal friend; and since he is leaving, I do not know what more I can do than to await his much-desired return, which I pray God will hasten, and I shall have to pray that he has good fortune. And, finally, since I see that Fortune wishes to test how loyal I am to Love, I shall endure this suffering, proving myself steadfast and unwavering, praying to Love that, if he has ever done anything at the request of one of his servants, he will want to respond to my sovereign desire by bringing back the most noble knight, [p. 127] who has put his life at risk and himself in danger of death many times in order to save my honor.'

48. *How Cligés arrived in Wallingford and went to a tournament that King Arthur's men were holding*

Of Fenice's regrets we shall make no more mention, for it is time to speak of Cligés, who traveled so far by land and sea that he arrived in Wallingford, a city in Great Britain. Then he asked after the king, and, when assured that

[30] Three lines were left blank here for the chapter title.
[31] In the context of *fin'amor*, the loyal lover considers the beloved to be the master or mistress of his or her heart and body.

he was very nearby in the city of Oxford to hold a tournament, he, who asked for nothing better, had three different sets of arms made, namely, the first black, the second green, and the third vermilion. Thus, along with the ones he had had in the battle against the duke of Saxony, which were white like an elephant bone, he had four sets, and four steeds, of which he later made very good use.

For on the first day of the tournament, when he had heard that the knights were going to begin to joust, he armed himself and headed for Oxford by the paths that his host had shown him. When he had arrived on the field and had seen approaching him the two parties that were to joust against each other, he directed himself toward the weaker, but he had barely arrived when Sagramors came out on the field to joust, for each day there was a prize given to the knight who performed the best on the lance attack. Sagramors was tall, strong, and feared, so there was no knight who dared to fight him. Cligés saw that no one made a move, so he told himself that he would not remain there [p. 128] without receiving a lance blow from Sagramors; so immediately he spurred on his black steed, and couched his lance, and settled himself firmly in his stirrups, and then he went forth to begin the joust.

49. How Cligés vanquished Sagramors and threw him to the ground

Sagramors saw Cligés clad in black armor coming toward him and went forward to meet him. At the attack, they delivered such great blows against each other that their lances failed, and Sagramors was unhorsed, which won everyone's praise for Cligés. Next appeared Aguichans, the king of Scotland, who struck him on the shield with his lance, but it broke, and Cligés went to strike him with all his might and with such speed that he felled both the knight and his horse.

Then there began a great clamor around Aguichans, and from all sides knights emerged breaking and destroying lances, shields, helmets, and hauberks. Plenty of knights were brought to the ground, and when lances were broken, suddenly swords were seized and great acts of prowess achieved with them. Cligés held his firmly and rushed into the thick of the fray, making the ranks tremble, and it seemed that there was no one like him in the world, and there was no man who on seeing him wanted to attack him one on one. Guivret le Petit saw him fighting thus and wanted to confront him; so he brought together four other knights and they surrounded Cligés on all sides and attacked him. Cligés, seeing himself surprised and surrounded, spurred his good steed and made the first, second, and third knights kiss the field, and he scattered the company so much that the boldest fled, leaving him alone. Thus, Cligés remained behind not knowing with whom he could fight. The tournament ended with praise being bestowed on the knight with the black armor. Seeing that all was over, Cligés left the field and returned to his lodging, then put his black armor out of sight, and displayed the green armor, so as not to be recognized.

[p. 129] 50. *How Cligés felled Lancelot du Lac in a course of lances*

When evening came, there was talk of no one except the knight with the black armor. The king sent men to seek him out, but no one could find out anything, which amazed him, and the next day, when everyone was ready to joust, Lancelot du Lac sallied forth, and he had barely arrived when Cligés, clad in green armor, came rushing on to the field on the attack. He saw Lancelot waiting and said to himself that he would test him and that he would not win the prize without striking a blow, so he sprang into action and everyone who saw him judged and testified that this one clad in the green armor seemed every bit as skilled as the one with the black arms who had appeared the day before. What more can I tell you? As soon as Lancelot du Lac saw Cligés couch his lance, he likewise couched his, then they came together so chivalrously that Lancelot split his lance, and Cligés came up against Lancelot's shield with such force that he pierced it through, then he raised it a little, and, employing all his might, shoved him to the ground. Everyone was amazed and said that it had been a long time since they had seen a knight of greater skill arrive at court.

After this, the two parties came together, and there is no need to inquire about the exploits of many noble knights who held their own most valiantly, but Cligés achieved the greatest renown, and there remained no man struck by his hand that he did not unhorse. Consequently, the best knights, seeing that they could do nothing against Cligés, left off jousting and retreated such that Cligés remained all alone. Then he set out and returned to his host secretly, placing the vermilion armor at the door of his lodging.

[p. 130] 51. *How Cligés beat Perceval le Galois*

Just as they had the day before, people spoke of noble Cligés's deeds, and that night no one spoke of anyone but the knight with the green armor, and, on the following day when it came time to joust, Cligés, now clad in his vermilion armor, was on the field, where Perceval le Galois was waiting for the first chivalric exploit. Then Cligés, who wanted to shine, after seeing that no one attacked this knight, spurred his horse, and striving as much as he could, headed toward Perceval and gave him such a blow with his lance that he knocked him down and caused both knight and horse to land in a heap.

Then you should have seen the other knights line up, couch their lances, and meet and strike each other so violently that one could see only lances breaking, shields splitting, and knights falling to the ground. The knights of the Round Table saw Cligés performing marvelous deeds, and they assembled and came against him on all sides, but, however hard they tried to strike him, Cligés held out his shield to them and exposed his hauberk, against which they could do no more than against a thick cement tower, and there was no man who could subjugate or dislodge him. When for a time he had suffered and endured the knights' blows, he conceived a sudden desire to fight, and he began to strike out so much with his sword that he freed himself from all those around him. With this deliverance the tournament ended.

Cligés returned to his lodging, and King Arthur to his court; and when the king realized that the knight with the green arms and the one with the black arms had not returned to the tournament, he thought about their performance and that of the knight with the vermilion arms that day, and he realized that it was a single knight who was amusing himself by making these changes so that he would not be recognized. And the king begged Sir Gauvain to undertake the first joust for the next day in order [p. 131] to test this knight. Sir Gauvain replied that he would do so willingly, although he suspected that he would be felled on the lance attack, but then he had hope that, if it came to fighting with the sword, he would let him know who he was.

Night passed and, the next day, when all had donned their armor, Sir Gauvain waited eagerly to joust. And all of a sudden Cligés, clad in his white armor and mounted on the white Arabian steed, arrived whirling about rapidly. He entered the field looking all around and, as soon as he saw Sir Gauvain ready to joust, he lowered his lance and rushed toward him. And Sir Gauvain, spurring his horse, came to meet him. With such speed did the two knights urge on their steeds that they seemed to be lifted into the air. And when they had to lower and break their lances, they did not fail at the attack. They broke lances, bridles, straps, breastplates, and reins, and both men necessarily fell to the ground. They got up skillfully, grabbing their bright, shiny, burnished swords, then without delay they went forward to strike each other, and a joust began between them that was very fierce and hard to sustain. For Sir Gauvain was very excited and desirous to do well in order to try Cligés, who was so valiant that among all the best knights all over the world he could be considered undeniably noble and courteous and handy with a sword. Then Cligés thought about his beautiful lady Fenice, which exalted his spirit, and he fought so well that Sir Gauvain could not defeat him, however much effort or work he put into it.

52. How Cligés revealed his identity to the king and to Gauvain

While King Arthur and his men saw them fighting, they drew closer and stopped to watch them, and, [p. 132] judging from the excellent form they saw in these two, they acknowledged that here were two knights of supreme skill. For they assailed each other and, employing several types of sword-play, they split and cleaved and smashed to pieces their good shields, and moreover the blows they struck on their helmets caused their swords to rebound, swerve, and spark fire, so violently did they clash, such that the king could not decide which was the better. And because he did not want to see either one vanquished, and as he saw Cligés displaying such expert swordplay – and indeed seemed no more fatigued at the end than at the beginning – he did not want their joust to continue. So he made them stop and told Sir Gauvain to make peace with the knight and thank him and ask him to come relax with him at court. Sir Gauvain did as the king ordered, and when Cligés agreed to go to the court, Sir Gauvain was very pleased.

The joust ended so that they could welcome Cligés of the white armor, who sent his squire to get him his robe, hat, belt, stockings, shoes, and other articles of clothing. Cligés was disarmed and, and his squire, having already arrived, dressed him in clothes styled like those of the Bretons. He entered the hall, and on his arrival, everyone ran up to him and, although they had never seen him with his face uncovered, as soon as he stood in the hall, because of his beauty he was recognized without any question as the knight who had performed so well.

There is no need for me to recount the great welcome that the king, Sir Gauvain, and all the other knights in general bestowed on him, but it is very proper to mention that the king and Sir Gauvain took him by the hand and, after [p. 133] looking closely at him, they implored him to tell them if he knew anything about the knights with the vermilion, black, and green armor who had jousted on the preceding days. Cligés, who saw that he was obliged and pressed to acknowledge what he had done, told them the truth, adding that he was the son of Alixandre and Soredamors. Of this the king was never so joyful, nor was Sir Gauvain. They kissed and embraced him affectionately, and the queen did likewise, then they offered him all their goods and loved him as dearly as if he were their own child, and the king gave him knights and squires to serve him, with a great many dogs and birds for his amusement and to pass the time. He used them for his diversion, indulging for many days in the noble sport of hunting and hawking.

53. How Cligés found a lady in a solitary place weeping about her beloved, who had gone away

So Cligés spent his youthful days seeking out jousts, tourneys, and other cer-emonies or prescribed activities related to the noble trade of arms, traveling through so many countries and regions that it would be too long to recount, where he increased his reputation considerably. And it happened one day while he was hunting deep in a wood that Fortune led and guided him so far in that he could find neither track nor path. For very few people frequented this wood as it was far from towns and houses; it was in fact a kind of wilderness, and there were only two or three main paths by which people could pass to go from one town to the next. When Cligés found himself there all alone, for his men were quite far behind him hunting wild game, he did not know what to think and would very much like to have been in their company.

In any case, he began to listen, hoping to hear something; [p. 134] thereupon, he became aware of a young lady weeping in a solitary place or hermitage, who began to cry out loudly in the following way, thinking that no one would hear her: 'Alas, God, who will be able to offer a single ray of hope to me, a woman deprived of all joy and felicity, who goes along weeping most of the days of her life in this wood as if lost and the only one grieving about her love? Alas, is there a sorrow greater that is comparable to my unique one? No, certainly not, and so I consider myself the most wretched and, among all those complaining about their misfortune and sorrowful life, the lady who most bitterly laments the loss of her dear beloved, who left her of late to go off in search of adventure. Now, I don't know if he is dead or alive or if he has found a love other than me, which would cause him to care nothing about ever returning. Oh, if only he had known my desire when he left. Alas, if I had revealed it to him, he would not have gone away, but maybe he will come back when it pleases God that I have done enough penance in this wood to merit obtaining his love. Now I have become a fugitive, for they wanted to marry me off, and I must stay here against my will until I receive some good news, for I dare not return to my country. So it must be said that I am that poor maiden exiled from all good things because of the departure of the very noble knight in pursuit of whom I recently sent my deputy, who has not come back. Alas! May God restore him – and joy – to me, as faithfully as he knows that my sorrow desires and yearns for him.' With that, the maiden fell silent.

And Cligés, who marveled at hearing that voice, felt pity for her and sought her until he [p. 135] found her in a great, massive thicket. Within there was a bower in which she sat combing her beautiful blond hair. Upon approaching, Cligés bowed, and she did likewise, feeling totally ashamed to see this man who had found her, and she cried out, 'Ha! Sir knight, have mercy on me and, for the love of God, keep safe the honor of this aggrieved maiden who, while awaiting news of a knight who is her beloved, weeps day and night begging that he return or that God deliver her on to death if he does not return. For it is the greatest good that I wish to have if He does not deliver me from this contemplative life and troubling exile.'

'Have no fear, my lady,' said Cligés, 'for, I swear to God on my soul that I would rather be dead than to have imagined or thought of bringing blame to you. Rather, for the love of the ladies, I would like to serve and honor you if you wish, like one who recognizes your loyalty in Love toward your beloved, to whom may God grant good fortune. Be comforted, my fair friend, and rest assured that God will come to your aid, for He is just and reasonable. I would like to know who you are and the name of your beloved so that I, who have long served King Arthur, might give you news of him if I have any.'

The maiden, quick to answer, told him the name of her beloved. Cligés had certain knowledge of him and said much good about him. 'But, sir knight,' said the maiden, 'please excuse me, and in this regard, in order to explain my situation, I shall tell you that I, weeping (as I said) over my beloved – the good knight about whom you have given me good news – am of royal lineage and have vowed never to reveal my name, situation, or country to anyone until God has helped me. For I am sought daily by [p. 136] men serving a king who wishes to marry me, in spite of me and against my will, because my father has agreed to it. And may God keep me from consenting, for never will it happen that my heart will fail in its promise to my eyes, which several times have invited my beloved to speak of what is most dear to his heart; of this I am quite certain. And rest assured that no one knows my hiding place except one of my relatives, a loyal squire who has gone off to recount what has befallen me to my beloved, whom I pray God will preserve.'

With this response Cligés was well pleased. He comforted the maiden with many kind words and, pensive and troubled, he left her and proceeded to return to his men by following the sound of the dogs that he heard barking and baying. But before he rejoined his men, he ventured to say the following words: 'Oh, how fine is the love of a good and loyal woman toward the one to whom she is devoted! I confess that this maiden's tears are worthy of great merit, indeed of as great a reward as the tears of a man who is loyal in Love's service. Alas! From what she said about having summoned her beloved by her sweet gaze, I can understand that Fenice, by means of her eyes, invited me to love her, for I do not believe that it is without reason that I am languishing every day for love of her, and now I recall Thessala who, on the day that Fenice wed my uncle, greeted me gladly and gave me a drink that I served him. In handing it to me, Thessala told me that if he tasted it, it would be better for me with regard to a certain lady. And I do not know what to think about this, except that it seems to me now, when I reflect on it, that Fenice always had her eye on me, so that, considering the ways that women find in matters of love, I must say that she loves me. [p. 137] Alas! Now, I have had no news of her for a long time, and, if she has been behaving like this other maiden, I would have to die of distress, for all the pain that I would have heard it said that she has endured would cause my heart such anguish that I would not be able to resist death, if Love's powers did not work within me and demonstrate their force. And for this reason, never will I linger in any place night or day until I have seen my lady and told her what is in my heart.'

On saying these words, Cligés rejoined his squires, and then leaving them behind, he rode from there until he came to King Arthur's court. He took leave of the king, queen, and Sir Gauvain, and everyone else, saying that he wanted to return for a while to his country. When he had prepared what he needed for his journey, he set out to sea and arrived with a good company of men at the port of Constantinople and made his arrival known to his uncle the emperor, who felt great joy, as did his people. But greater still was the joy of the empress Fenice, who, languishing shortly before, was soon able to nourish her loyal heart by means of a single look at Cligés.

54. *How the emperor and Fenice went to greet Cligés*

Cligés had not yet entered the city when the emperor and Fenice, with all the barons, came to greet him. He kissed [p. 138] Fenice sweetly, a kiss she did not refuse; indeed, she served Cligés with a deep sigh as their two mouths met. And after this Cligés, well versed in courtly matters, went to embrace and kiss all the ladies and maidens, who bowed nicely to him, and each welcomed him nobly as was appropriate. Then he was led and conducted with great solemnity to the palace. The emperor increased the court's joy by holding a round table for all comers.

But our account falls silent regarding the entertainment, friendly greetings, dinners, and suppers that characterized this welcome and proceeds to speak of Cligés and Fenice, who could not keep from turning their gaze toward each other. Many times Cligés found himself alone with Fenice, for the emperor suspected nothing, but now Cligés did not know what to do. He dared not reveal his thoughts to his most beloved lady for fear of offending and being refused by Fenice; for that reason he did not know how to act, so great was his discomfort. For a long time he was languishing for the love of this beauty, who had no less pain than he.

And after a while, one day among others, this loyal servant Cligés happened to find himself in Fenice's chamber where she was alone. After an exchange of greetings, she took him by the hand, and they withdrew to a remote window to speak of what concerned them. And first, after asking him about his trip to Britain and how the king and princes were, when it came to speaking of the queen, the ladies, and the maidens, she asked him if he had not seen a lady to whom he had given his heart.

'Alas, my lady,' said Cligés, 'I would have done so with great difficulty, for, since leaving you, my heart has not kept me company; rather, when my body left, my heart remained behind, namely with you, my cherished lady. And because I could not [p. 139] dwell in Britain, given the separation of my heart from my body, I had to come back to this land with all haste to see if I could recover it. Now you, my lady, if you please, tell me what you think of this empire, and if you are happy here and have been so up to now, for, although it is not my business, nevertheless I, within my limited faculty and power, would be very happy to know you are well, and if you should need anything that I could supply, I would do so gladly and willingly.'

55. *How Fenice answered Cligés with respect to her love*

'Certainly, Cligés, my most beloved knight,' said Fenice, 'there is no need to inquire about my joy or my pleasure, for there has been none and, if your body had not returned here, I know well that my heart would have perished and died promptly. For this heart, which shortly before was sighing and lamenting about you, could not recover its joy except by the means I found in gazing at you. And thank God, since you have confessed that your heart has always been with me, I can certainly say that it is mine, and regarding mine you can also consider that it is more than yours, because of the unexpected and good friendship by which Love has joined the two and made them so devoted to each other that mine is yours and yours is mine. So I can consider myself the happiest of women, since Love has transformed our two hearts, joining them in a loyal cause and firm will, such that I have never been inclined to love any man but you, starting from the first day that your uncle wed me against my will. But, thanks to a drink that you gave him, he has never had carnal knowledge of me. Rather, because of the good things [p. 140] I had heard about you, who should rightly wear the emperor's crown, and in consideration of your surpassing beauty, goodness, prowess, and nobility, I decided and resolved to love no one but you during my lifetime. In this way I kept myself chaste, hoping to have better. Therefore, my friend Cligés, I beg you to think about our situation, which will be sustained at God's pleasure, with my honor safe; for nothing else do I desire.'

56. *How Fenice and Cligés spoke of several things, and Fenice decided to pretend she was dead*

'My most honored lady,' said Cligés, 'although I am not worthy enough to be in your good graces, nevertheless, since you should be mine through the arrangement by which you were given in marriage to the emperor of Constantinople (whose crown I should wear), and since my service is agreeable to you, I thank God for such good fortune. And since it pleases God and Love that our loyal friendship be secretly and firmly sustained, it seems to me, if I am not mistaken, that it would be good if I took you to Britain, for I am certain that you would be received there with greater joy than was beautiful Helen by the Trojans when Paris ravished her and took her off. And so that I should not be considered negligent and remiss in my affairs, as for myself, I am ready to do anything you say or propose.'

'Oh, my beloved,' said Fenice, 'we will have to find another solution, for if you took me away, people all over the world would speak of us as they did of Yseult and Tristan, and, on my honor, I would be most unhappy if that happened, and there would be [p. 141] no one who would not deem or consider me most shameless and you quite mad. Rather, so that our love may persist, I shall tell you what we shall do. For my part, I shall feign illness, and eventually death, and during this fictional illness, you will have a coffin made in such a way that there will be a hole through which I shall have air when I am placed inside. And, afterwards, in the evening you will come and get me in secret and incognito to take me away with you. I shall be neither lady nor empress if you are not lord and emperor. For if, according to my plan, I am taken by you to a place where no one will recognize me, I shall be the happiest lady in the world.'

'My lady,' said Cligés, 'may God be praised for your good sense and ruse. It seems to me that your proposal is subtly and well fashioned. If you consult with your nurse Thessala about this, and if she advises you to do it, the most sensible thing for us to do will be to do it quickly. And with regard to the coffin, there will be no problem, for in this city I have a serf who was sold to me some time ago and who is the most skillful who exists under heaven. For there is no worker anywhere who is his equal, and I shall test him first, and if for good pay he agrees to keep the secret, once I have received his pledge, I shall put him to work, if it should please you.'

57. *How Thessala promised Fenice to give her a sleeping potion that would cause her to appear dead*

'Cligés, my beloved,' said the lady, 'all that you arrange I shall consider well done, and I have such confidence in you that I shall leave everything up to you.' Then the two lovers took leave of each other. Cligés left while Fenice remained. She summoned her nurse Thessala, and once she was there, Fenice took her aside and said, 'Look now, Nurse, it is true that I trust you because I feel that you are loyal and discreet, and you know [p. 142] rather a lot about my illness – that nothing can comfort my young heart if Cligés, with his sweet words and his noble feelings is not present before me. And there is nothing that gives my eyes more joy than seeing that one person, Cligés, who loves me as I love him, and in fact he has courted me such that for his love I have resolved with him to pretend to be infirm, sick, and to feign death. So it would be good that if you know of some way to help me, you should show me, for without your knowledge I cannot carry out my plan. Therefore, I should like very much to entreat you to make pledges, covenants, and oaths to help me with all my affairs and to be loyal toward me and my beloved.'

'My dearest child,' said Thessala, 'it is not by me that your plan will be hindered, and right now I swear on my soul, God, and all the saints – male and female – that since I must be involved I will accomplish my task so well that you will be content with my diligence. And I will make you such a drink that no man who sees you will dare to say or affirm that life has not left you, for it will have such power that it will make you cold, pale, and weak so that neither pulse nor breath will be detected in you for the length of one day and one night. During that time, everyone will think for sure that you are deprived of soul and life, by which our enterprise will meet a good end, if it should please God.'

58[32]

'Fair nurse,' said Fenice, 'I thank you. For my part, heeding your words, I commit myself totally to [p. 143] doing what your good discretion should order and, because I wish to set in motion and implement what I desire, you will say to my women – both ladies and maidens – who see me in this room that I am not very well.'

A great number had long since come, and knights as well. Fenice pretended to be ill and ordered her bed to be prepared. She had hardly finished speaking when Thessala stood up and made a show of being irritated. Pulling a sad face, she went before the ladies, saying, 'Now, quickly, knights, ladies, and maidens, please leave, for my lady is unwell, and as she wishes to take care of herself she has ordered that you should go to another room so that she can rest a while.' With these words, everyone left, manifesting an unaccustomed and very anguished sorrow.

But our account will fall silent regarding the tears they showed and now speak of Cligés's conduct toward his worker.[33]

59. How Cligés presented his case to his worker Jehan, who promised to be discreet

The story relates that after leaving Fenice Cligés sought out Jehan, his mason and carpenter, until he found him and brought him to a secret place, then told him the following: 'My friend and my man, Jehan, you who know how to do all manner of things, for the great reputation that you have throughout the world, and also because you are my serf, by which you owe me faith and loyalty, I have sent for you in all confidence to execute a project that I have undertaken. But before I tell you, you will swear to me and take an oath, and I shall promise to do so much good by you that you and your lineage will prosper.'

At these words, Jehan raised his hand to the saints, [p. 144] swearing to accomplish stealthily whatever things were commanded of him, without any reservations, truly, if it should be in his power. 'And so,' he said, 'tell me your plan and, by the faith that I owe you, I will willingly devote myself to accomplishing it.'

'Then,' said Cligés to his worker, 'since you assure me that you will not reveal what I tell you, truly – and this I hardly dare put into words – I shall in all confidence inform you of my plan. It is that you must make me a coffin beautifully crafted in such a way that whoever is placed inside will never

---

[32] The title that is found here in the manuscript should be at the beginning of the following chapter.
[33] A small red decoration completes the last line of the chapter. The break is confirmed by the large red 'D' [Dist] that follows.

perish there but rather will have enough air. For, my friend, it will receive the body of Fenice, who by right belongs to me in many respects, and who will feign death for love of me; and once she has been placed in the coffin that I have described, I shall be able, if it please God, to remove her by good means and carry her off to a foreign land.'

'I will certainly be able to accomplish this work,' said Jehan, 'but never will there be any need to take her anywhere but to your house, the one that you gave me some time ago, if you'd like. For it is as pleasant there as any place where a lady might be taken.'

'Let's go, then,' said Cligés, 'and if the place is such as you describe, you will gain even more by it.'

Then they went into the house, which was adjacent to the city walls, and Jehan took Cligés into rooms adorned with windows and painted in gold, blue, silver, green, violet, crimson – indeed, in all colors – then he led him into a sanctuary by a narrow passage that they soon located, and it was well made and suitable for ladies or maidens. This place had a door made of a great slab of marble painted like white stone and with such subtlety that no man would have been able to say that there was an opening in this wall. Nevertheless, Jehan opened it, which caused Cligés to marvel. When they were inside, they found beautiful fountains, sweet and clear like silver, [p. 145] made of porphyry in the form of pipes carved in more than a hundred different shapes representing various beasts and birds, from whose mouths gushed the water of these fountains and from which issued a small river that flowed into another one underground. Next they found baths, tubs, pools, clear and pleasant vaulted chambers furnished with curtained beds and looms for working silk where no type of material in the world was lacking, for they were provided with all of them.

And if anyone were ever to ask me how this man had been able to make this place so pleasant all by himself without anyone's help, and indeed had decorated it so splendidly that nothing more beautiful could be made, the story explains that the worker, who was clever, had found in this house a silver mine whose sale had enabled him to live eight whole years without devoting himself to anything but his work; moreover, he had found this place already vaulted so that he needed only to decorate it and make subtle changes in order finally to be freed from the condition of servitude where he found himself. And he has accomplished this, for his effort has now been turned to good effect.

Cligés was delighted to have found this pleasant place, manor, and dwelling. He freed Jehan and granted him all that he might ask for, begging him to make the coffin quickly and to do everything in his power to help him carry out his project until his lady could be installed within. Jehan said that this presented no obstacle and assured him that he would help him with this if his knowledge were sufficient to the task. Then he immediately began to craft, carve, and assemble strongly and securely this coffin, which could also be called a tomb.

Cligés left him and went to the palace, where he found everyone manifesting great sorrow because they thought that Fenice was ill, for she had [p. 146] prohibited anyone from entering her chamber except for the emperor and Cligés, to whom she would not have dared to refuse entry, as she said.

60. How Cligés spoke to Fenice, as she lay in bed, about what he had arranged with Jehan

The murmuring and lamentations that Cligés heard around him mattered little to him, for he knew well the malady that was the cause of this weeping. He banged on the door of Fenice's chamber, and old Thessala opened the door for him, and Cligés, who found his lady in bed, greeted her, and after a few long looks, told her how he had negotiated with his worker. Fenice was very pleased and, when they had made several decisions, in order that nothing could be perceived to be amiss she began to cry aloud, 'Cligés, please take leave of me, for my sickness is so severe and painful that I could no longer stand for you to be in my presence.'

On hearing these words, Cligés, who knew full well how to fake affliction, departed, mournful in appearance but joyful in reality, and it certainly seemed, for whoever saw him, that he was the most discomfited among them, owing to the sorrowful countenance with which he concealed the perfect happiness he felt on seeing that his beautiful beloved knew well how to play her role. She gesticulated and frequently flailed about on one side and the other. The emperor rushed to her, and when he saw her pale and complaining of pain in all her limbs and not wanting a thing to eat, he began to weep and asked her if he should send for doctors.

'Doctors? God!' said Fenice. 'Alas, sire, are you so sick of my life that you want to deliver me into the hands of those who, greedy for your money, will cause me to die? On my faith, never will a man minister to me other than the only one who can make me live or die and by whom I shall be able to escape from this grievous suffering if he wills it. Or, if not, I shall patiently accept what it pleases him to send me, for I shall have to die some day.' When the emperor heard Fenice's words, he thought she was awaiting [p. 147] the will of God, who does what He wishes with each one, but these words have a double meaning: for the emperor understands God, whereas Fenice means Cligés, whom she considers and covertly names her doctor, which he truly is.

61. How Thessala took the urine of an old woman and showed it to the emperor, telling him it was Fenice's

After imparting regrets and advice to Fenice, the emperor departed by her order, sad and sorrowful.

Now, there was in the city an old and very sick woman whom Thessala went to visit every day while Fenice pretended to be ill, and one of these times, she went one morning to see her and took a sample of her urine and thus realized that she would die before nightfall. She pretended to throw it out but kept it and went back to tell Fenice how she had taken a urine sample from the old woman who would die that day. Fenice was very pleased, and ordered her to go and show it to her husband the emperor. On Fenice's order, Thessala went to show this urine sample to the emperor, who summoned doctors to examine it. Once they had come, he asked them to tell him what they could conclude about Fenice's illness. They answered that Fenice was close to death, and that she would never live beyond nones of that day.

Oh, what harsh news for this sorrowful emperor! He fainted straightaway, as did most of his barons as well, and they lamented with grief and tender tears, whereas Thessala, who saw that she had work to do, departed and slyly went off to prepare her brew. At about the twelfth hour that it [p. 148] had been brewing, Fenice, in the emperor's presence, asked for a drink. Thessala brought some of this brew, which she served her, and about half an hour later, when the drink had produced its effect within her, heaving many sighs, she closed her eyes and mouth, then became pale and cold and extended her feet, arms, and legs as though she were dead, which caused the emperor to faint many times.

62. *How the emperor complained to God about Death*

As soon as Fenice was asleep, as described above, the news was published and related in many places that she was dead, and never have there been made such anguished lamentations, especially by the emperor who does not know what to do, but strikes his heart with his fists, and with wild chagrin begins to make the following complaint: 'Oh, most wretched man! How will your heart bear seeing your beloved lady dead without bursting from sorrow and splitting from painful memory? Oh, Fortune, what have you done to me by leaving me deprived of, and separated, exiled, and banished from my sovereign worldly pleasure! Alas, alas! True and good God, how have I offended Your divinity for You to allow harsh, cruel, inhuman, inconstant, and abominable Death to kill my joy, solace, happiness, and this beautiful lady, the sight of whose most excellent beauty kept me alive!'

On saying these words, he falls to the ground as though half dead, along with the palace retinue, knights, ladies, and maidens, affected by this new and unaccustomed regime of sadness. Beating their breasts they begin to make this complaint against Death: 'Death, oh Death, what moves you to inflict on us this contrary and untimely plague? You are too eager to do wrong by depriving us of the best tempered of all women! Oh, unhappy You, the God who governs all and watches over all good creatures, [p. 149] it is a marvel how You have allowed the heart of a princess of such high rank and perfect moral qualities to expire through outrageous Death, which, given this great loss, deserves to be considered a cruel murderer since it has disfigured the noblest work that Nature has ever produced.'

63. How three doctors, passing through Constantinople and seeing the people weeping, inquired about their grief

In the midst of the tears, cries, weeping, sighs, and lamentations that the emperor, the ladies, and the common people were making over Fenice's death, there arrived before the palace of Constantinople old, white-haired physicians coming from Salerno. Seeing the court and the whole place full of grieving people, they stopped and inquired as to why they were weeping and crying in great confusion, saying, 'Oh, you heart-broken people, tell us if you please why you are mourning in such anguish so that we, passing through, might feel the pain that you bear and add our sighs, if it is suitable.'

'You who are passing along this path,' answered the people of Constantinople, 'wait and see if there exists a sorrow comparable to ours, and, since you inquire about the moaning that we make, in order that you not think that it is without cause that we wring our aggrieved limbs in this common labor, we reply that good reason moves us to do so. For crazy and most frenzied Death has this day wrongly inflicted on us such a loss that with its bloody and poisonous dart made with fatal venom it has pierced through the heart of our good and noble princess in whose body God and Nature had put so much light that in the entire feminine sex, as vast as it is, there is no one like her. [p. 150] So our eyes are not tear-stained without good reason, nor are our hearts joined in a communal act of weeping without cause, nor are they unjustly in revolt against Death, nor are we wrong to complain about this misfortune, for in our lady there reposed beauty, humility, refinement, generosity, and all the gifts of wisdom.'

Hearing this response the doctors are very afflicted, and they state that they will go see the lady, saying that if she is not absolutely and unremittingly deceased they will restore her to health. They advance and with the emperor's permission they approach Fenice's body, which is already in a shroud, and tap it in many places and say to one another that she is not dead. And there is one, the most expert in medicine, who proclaims to the emperor, 'Sire, take comfort, by my word, cease your oppressed weeping, for I swear by my head that your wife is not dead and that I shall restore her to life for you before she escapes from my hands.'

64. How the doctors spoke to Fenice and removed her from the coffin

Now the mourning and wailing have diminished, and each one lends an ear to learn what the emperor and the physicians will command. At the words of the old physician, the emperor raises his face that was bowed in sadness and with sad words he says to him, 'You, who exhort me to take comfort, claiming that my wife has not passed from this world, you present me with a great marvel. Take care what you say, for if you cannot prove what you have reported in my presence, great misfortune will be yours. May God give you grace to work well, and, if it turns out to be as you have told me, I shall make you a rich man and give you the greater part of my treasury; but if not, [p. 151] I shall have you burned alive or hanged.'

'Sire,' says the doctor with the hoary beard, 'I accept the terms that you have given me, but now, everyone must vacate this place except for my two companions who will help me in my undertaking.'

The emperor is pleased and has everyone leave the place, and he him-self goes out, which Cligés would have willingly advised against, if he had dared; and thus the three physicians remain with Fenice. But Love will keep them from making the lady speak, and, for the distress they will cause her, he, as judge, will make them die a deserved and villainous death.

When they have closed and locked the door, they approach the lady, and first of all, without knives or razors but with brute force they remove her from her coffin, tearing the shroud in which she is wrapped. Then, since they are sure she is feigning death, they speak to her in this manner: 'Lady, you who are pretending to be dead, rise up and speak to us in all confidence, for we are certain that you are alive. So be assured that you will not escape by this means, notwithstanding, however, that we have pity on your fresh, tender, and pleasing flesh, and it would be a shame if in the flower of your age you were to be buried after dying in a rage from some unpleasant thing that has been inflicted on you. And for this reason, if you wish to speak and open your eyes, all three of us assure you that we shall help you cover up your ruse as best we can, promising to preserve your honor in all cases.'

65. How the doctors beat Fenice with their belts

The old men speak thus to Fenice, believing that by their covert cajoling words she will be willing to be won over, but all is in vain, for she is aided by Love, who so admonishes her not to move that they cannot get a single word out of her. So they begin to torture her horribly, punching and slap-ping her so much that it is awful to hear the blows they deliver. To be brief, they grow tired of striking [p. 152] this beautiful lady who becomes black from being beaten, and, resorting again to words, they heckle her, saying that if she does not surrender they will torment her using the most grievous punishment with which any woman was ever tortured. The more her doc-tors speak, the less Fenice takes heed; so they remove their belts and begin to strike this lady cruelly, and so much do they beat her front and back that blood runs rapidly, flows, and streams from every part of her. Despite this assault and harsh torture, Fenice does not move but rather maintains herself so firmly that she seems much more dead than alive.

66. *How the doctors poured molten lead into Fenice's palms*

After the great torment that the wicked doctors have made beautiful Fenice endure, it is not enough to have torn her fresh, white, tender flesh, but in addition they take lead that they melt in a little vessel, and when it is so hot that it is boiling, they pour it into Fenice's palms. She suffers this torture with great difficulty, but she sustains it by Love's encouragement. When they see that this is not working, they melt some oil on her chest and after that torture they prepare a grate, put a large coal fire underneath, and say with great inhumanity, like wicked, indecent, old, white-haired, and merciless men that they will roast Fenice or make her talk.

They had already placed Fenice on the grate when the ladies, thinking that the doctors were taking too long to accomplish their task, peeked through a small crack in the door and saw that the doctors intended to roast Fenice. Overcome with rage, they screamed at the doctors and pounded and kicked the door so hard that they broke it down and entered the room. God knows what great pity they felt on seeing Fenice suffer the flames and heat of the coals as though dead.

[p. 153] 67. *How the ladies made the doctors jump out the windows, killing them*

As described above, the ladies broke down the door of the room, and Thessala, seeing Fenice, ran to her and embraced her, weeping profusely, and restored her somewhat, while the other ladies and maidens approached the three doctors. They assailed them mightily, scratching their withered faces, pulling out their white hair, twisting their grey beards, and, after they had hit them and crushed them against the walls, they took them by the shoulders and made them jump out the high windows and fall to the ground below in such a way that, on falling, their feeble limbs weakened by old age were smashed and broken so that they died instantly and did not have a chance to make their excuses to the emperor, who had their bodies hung at the gallows.

Once the ladies had, with hasty deliberation, taken vengeance on the doctors, whose words and resistance were for naught, they applied ointment and fragrant oils to the body of Love's martyr, and once she was anointed and wrapped anew in the shroud up to her face, never had anyone seen greater mourning. The emperor and his sad company arrived then, reinforcing it with their wretched cries, and, if they had been sorrowful before, it was no comparison to what they were now.

68. *How Fenice was placed in a coffin and carried to the church*

What is the use of recounting further the cries that everyone made for love of Fenice? We shall leave the weeping Cligés, who does not know how Fenice is, and come to the [p. 154] point when the emperor sent Jehan to get a coffin and prepare her tomb well and elaborately. Jehan told him he would definitely provide him well with a coffin and all that he needed. He sent the coffin to the palace, and in all haste went off to craft the stone tomb where Fenice was to be put, and he placed the slab over it so skillfully that one would not have known if there was an opening or not.

After Jehan had prepared Fenice's tomb, and she was placed in the coffin, with all the bells of all the churches already ringing, she was brought to the church with a great spilling of tears. And when her service was finished and Jehan had put her in the stonework that we call a tomb, and the slab had already been placed on top, then was there twice as much affliction mani-fested by the emperor, ladies, and knights, who often fainted. Finally, they left her and began to return toward the palace, cursing that woeful day.

Even Cligés, who did not know how Fenice was faring, was in great distress and made such a great lamentation that with each sigh it seemed as though his soul would issue from his body, and it was a marvel that he did not kill himself. But nevertheless, however difficult it might be, he said he would wait until he had learned the truth about her, that is, until he had taken and removed her from the coffin and tomb at nightfall.

At dusk, the emperor sent thirty men-at-arms to keep vigil over the corpse, which put Cligés very ill at ease. But Love by his grace will come to his aid.

69. *How Cligés and Jehan went to take Fenice's body from the guard of thirty men-at-arms*

When the thirty men-at-arms were settled around Fenice's corpse, the em-peror sent them good wines and good meats, and [p. 155] a great coal fire was made, but as God wished, they drank so much wine and ate so copi-ously that they became drunk and one after the other they all fell asleep around eleven o'clock that night.

Now was Cligés deep in thought: he stole away from his men and as soon as he could he came to Jehan, his worker, to whom he related the presence of the thirty armed men. Jehan, on hearing this, armed Cligés in like manner so that those who had by chance fallen asleep and afterwards might awaken would not suspect him. Armed from head to foot, Cligés came to the gate accompanied by Jehan. He found it locked, but through an opening he could see everything inside, for there were plenty of candles and burning torches giving such great illumination that Cligés saw all the men-at-arms asleep. This gave him great hope, but he did not know how he could get inside.

Finally, he who can barely wait to see his beloved, rushes to the wall surrounding the church and, with the help of Love, who supports him, grips the wall so well that in little time he has both feet on it. Then, by means of a tree, he descends into the cemetery and covertly goes to open the gate for his worker Jehan, who goes inside. They turn to Fenice's sepulcher, and right in the midst of the thirty men-at-arms who are there, Jehan lifts the slab, and Cligés enters the tomb and takes Fenice out of the coffin and into his arms, and he is so joyful that he does not know whether he is dead or alive. He kisses and hugs her a hundred times and carries her from there. Jehan replaces the slab securely and skillfully. They leave rapidly and go out by the main gate, which they draw closed after them, leaving the cemetery guards sleeping because of their drunken state or by Love's commandment. Love does not want the martyr Fenice and her gracious friend Cligés to have labored in vain; rather, at [p. 156] this hour he wishes their undertaking to be completely secret, for Fenice is transported to Jehan's house without their meeting any obstacle.

Cligés was led by Jehan to the vaulted room where he set Fenice down, but he had not even caught his breath before he unwrapped Fenice's shroud and found her pale and livid, showing not the slightest sign of life. No one was more upset than Cligés, who thought she was dead and several times fell to the floor in a faint while covering her tender face with copious tears. Finally, he began to speak, uttering this lamentation.

70. *The lamentations that Cligés made against Death*

'Alas, most lofty power of Love, what is the place where my heart should turn in order to redeem, by grievous laments and acts of penitence, the death of my lady and sovereign mistress? Oh, what will happen to my grieving heart; who will sustain it, and what will it do, since I am forced to see with my own eyes my well-being, my love, and my delight transformed into terrible pain and despair because the object of my greatest desire has died a martyr's grievous death for love of me? You, Fortune, choose quickly the gloomy place where I shall repay, with interminable tears and cries, this great loss that has occurred because of me. Upon my faith, it is not possible for me to compensate in the least for this most wretched torture that my lady has endured because of me, since I would never be finished any day of my life with the sad custom of lamentation. Oh, Death, false, unjust, and disloyal Death, how greatly you have offended by vanquishing the loyal heart of the one who loved me so. Oh, Fortune, cruel deceiver, what do you wish to do with me since you sent the old men who killed my lady to be present at my greatest undertaking? I would have preferred that you had sent [p. 157] death to me instead and that she had remained alive.'

Upon saying these last words, Cligés faints, falling next to Fenice, who then makes a movement, and since the philter has lost its force, opens her eyes and on opening her mouth there issues from her such a great sigh; Cligés hears it and, although he is in a swoon, he suddenly raises his sorrowful face. He sees her but cannot speak, and Fenice, to whom the common style of speaking has been restored, moves her tongue to speak, wishing to comfort her sweet friend Cligés.

71. How Fenice comforted her friend Cligés

'My most loyal friend Cligés, I beg of you, look at me and, on noting that I have recovered my speech and wits, cease somewhat your lamentations, for, as much as I am in peril of death, this danger is not as hard on me as is the mourning that I have heard you make. And thanks be to God and Love, since I see myself here, and even though I must die, I am grateful for this misfortune and prefer to languish here with you than to live elsewhere.'

'Certainly, my lady,' said Cligés, 'I would not be able to find it in me to give my afflicted heart a single hour of rest until I know how you are faring.'

'Alas, my friend,' said Fenice, 'I feel so badly afflicted that I have no hope of escaping death, but, if my nurse could come minister to me, she knows so much about medicine that there is no physician in the world who knows more than she.'

'That will pose no obstacle,' said Cligés. He sent secretly for Thessala, who came before Fenice and, after kisses and greetings, promised to deliver her cured and healthy within two weeks' time. Then she took out her ointments, which she spread on Fenice as gently as she could and took such good care of her that on the thirteenth day [p. 158] Fenice was totally recovered and healthy. Cligés derived great joy from this, and every day he went there by night and day using as an excuse to enter this house the care of his falcon and other birds that he had put there. So there was no one who could notice what he was doing, for on the pretext of seeing his bird, he went to see his lady, who rejoiced greatly over his visits. Scarcely would she have wished to be in paradise because the great good to which she had aspired for such a long time was now given and granted to her.

72. How Fenice asked Cligés for an orchard

For more than a year, Fenice remained in the hidden place without going out, but as she sensed that the season was joyful, the winds were diminishing, and the birds were singing variously and melodiously because of the beautiful vestments they saw the trees donning through Nature's gifts, one morning she heard the nightingale singing at daybreak and chattering in its language. Now, she was with Cligés, but, although they were speaking of matters relating to Love, the nightingale's beautiful song made them interrupt their conversation, and the lady, as though exalted in spirit and with renewed joy, could not keep from saying to Cligés, 'Oh how subtle and marvelous is Nature, for, although I am in this place that is uninhabited and unfrequented except by you and me, I am moved in my natural feelings by the renewal of the season when beasts, which are not even endowed with understanding, consider the poverty they have suffered over the short days and long nights of winter. And for the good they hope to have, they rejoice in this beginning when the trees adorn themselves and put on greenery producing sweet and lovely flowers and little branches. So they force me to fix on an unaccustomed memory after my trials, tribulations, [p. 159] and ordeals, and it seems to me that never shall I need anything but an orchard of delights in which I could take comfort and pass time joyfully amid the harmonious songs of the birds.'

'My lady,' said Cligés, 'if it is possible to make one for you, I know well that Jehan will not fail me in this task. And because there is no pleasure in the world that I should not wish to provide for your heart, since I desire to increase your delight, I shall do my utmost to do so.'

73. How Cligés and Fenice entered the orchard of delights

Then Cligés went to find Jehan his worker and brought him before Fenice. Cligés asked him for an orchard, begging him for the love of Fenice to create one promptly. 'In truth,' said Jehan, 'I do not lack an orchard, as you will see shortly.' He led them through a well-built stone refuge to the orchard gate, and they had barely stepped inside when they beheld this pleasant spot[34] adorned with all kinds of flowers. In its center stood a grafted flowering tree, trained in such a way that the branches covered with greenery and beautiful flowers descended exactly to the earth, giving a lovely shade to a beautiful enclosed meadow that was situated all around the circumference or contour of the trunk for as far as the branches of the tree extended. And this meadow was covered with daisies watered by a stream coming from the fountains of the vaulted apartments. It flowed so beautifully that the water seemed silvery, and the two lovers had great delight in seeing this place that was serene, private, and better protected than any other. They went from plot to plot, from row to row visiting the beautiful little flowers, then they entered the meadow, and there they lay down embracing and kissing, each fulfilling the other's desire.

[p. 160] 74[35]

On that very day it happened that a knight named Bertrand went off after dinner to play in the fields and came straight up to the outer wall of the

---

[34] 'spot': proposed to fill a lacuna; Foerster, p. 335, supplied 'vergier' (= orchard), but as Co-lombo Timelli notes, p. 186, one could also propose 'lieu' (= place, spot).
[35] A blank space equivalent to three lines was no doubt intended for the chapter title.

garden where Cligés and Fenice were, and, finding a temporary distraction, he thought to entrust his bird to his page, from whom it escaped by chance and went to alight right on Jehan's house. Bertrand was very upset when he saw his bird escape, but he said in any case that he would not lose it and that if he could once get into the orchard, then his bird would respond easily to his call. He put his hands on the wall and, since he was agile, he leaped inside, and he had barely advanced when he saw Cligés and Fenice embracing each other under the flowering tree. He marveled at the sight and began to say to himself, 'Oh, what a strange imagination I have, for it seems to me in any case that I see Fenice with Cligés and, upon my soul, if she had not died and been buried over a year ago, I would say that it's she, for strictly speaking her extraordinarily beautiful face persuades me and decrees that it is Fenice in body and soul. So I don't know what this could be, and I have never in my life seen such a marvel.'

As he spoke these words, Fenice raised her face somewhat and quickly saw this knight Bernard who was looking at her attentively, and it filled her with shame. She pointed him out to her beloved, Cligés, who jumped up without a word and seized his good sword, which he had brought with him, and drew it out of the scabbard. Bertrand, on seeing Cligés striding toward him, turned his back, and he was already halfway up the wall and indeed had one leg outside when Cligés grabbed him, and because he could not reach his head he sliced clear through his leg. Bertrand fell all at once among his men, who were totally amazed when they saw that his leg had been severed. They picked him up with [p. 161] great dismay and bound his knee with a kerchief, then put him on a palfrey and inquired about his misadventure. But he replied that he would never recount it until he had told the emperor everything.

He headed for the palace, and when the people saw him with his damaged leg, which was still bleeding profusely, they all followed him until he was before the emperor to whom he related that he had seen his wife Fenice with Cligés, who had cut off his leg and had even tried to kill him. The emperor and his barons marveled at this news, and while someone, following orders, went to the tomb where they had put the empress to see if she was there, Thessala went off to Jehan's house and found Cligés and Fenice, who were already on horseback. Cligés hoisted Thessala up behind him and then they departed and went on their way with all haste.

Meanwhile, when nothing was found in Fenice's coffin, the emperor went off to Jehan's house and some of his people entered through the orchard and spent at least half the day looking for Cligés and Fenice, believing they were still there. But since they were not able to find them, the emperor had Jehan seized and swore he would cut off his head if he did not acknowledge the truth. When Jehan saw himself in the custody of the men-at-arms and heard the emperor threaten him with death, he related the entire story about Fenice from beginning to end. 'But,' he said, 'to you who are emperor without right or reason, so that you may know that I do not deserve to die, I declare that I am his serf, and that by right I could not and must not refuse him anything he requests of me. For first of all this house is his, and henceforth if there is someone who wishes to say or assert that my lord Cligés has wronged you, I am happy to risk my life to save my master's honor. And finally, if you wish to have me killed unjustly, before dying I will pardon my lord, saying that the ambassadors pledged [p. 162] and betrothed Fenice for and in the name of the emperor of Constantinople whose imperial jurisdiction by direct succession of endowed lineage is owed to Cligés. So wherever he is, he is its lord, although you have very wrongly disinherited both him and his father. And so that you could wear the crown, you had sworn and promised never to take a wife. Fenice mulled over these things in her heart, and, having heard the full story, resolved to offer herself to her true servant who, with Love's permission fell in love with her from the first time he ever saw her, and she with him, as God and Reason wished. And know that on your wedding day you were given a drink endowed with such power that you were barely in bed when you fell asleep and thought you were doing what you never did and never will do, and I will tell you no more about it; do with me what you wish.'

Oh, how distressed was the emperor when he heard these words! He had Jehan put in prison, saying that he would have him put to death along with Cligés, and there would be no city, town, castle, or fortress where he would not have Cligés sought and, if found, seized, indeed, and finally put to death. And then he dispatched and sent his men quickly after him, promising great gifts to those who would find him and bring him in. But one went off who would willingly help Cligés carry out his venture, if need be.

75. *How Cligés arrived at King Arthur's court and recounted his adventure with Fenice*

For as long as a month after the two lovers' departure, the Greeks did not stop seeking and searching for them, but Thessala conveyed them so secretly by enchantments that they were not found; rather, they went along safely without encountering anything worth relating until they arrived in London, in Britain, where King Arthur and his barons were. They had great joy at Cligés's arrival, but the king had even greater joy when he heard Fenice's story recounted. He said he would seek revenge [p. 163] for Emperor Alix's conduct and would go to Greece with such a huge army to restore Cligés to his imperial throne that his uncle would not dare to resist anywhere when faced with him.

He summoned his men and had already assembled a great army and prepared a very fine fleet of sailing ships, barques, galleys, and all sea-going vessels when messengers coming from Greece arrived there and asked so insistently for Cligés that they came into his presence where King Arthur was. They bowed to him as to their emperor. Then Jehan stepped forward and told him that his uncle Alix had died of frenzied grief after ascertaining the truth about him and Fenice. 'And because, my lord,' he said, 'the people of the country found that I had been loyal to you, they sent me with these noble barons to tell you that they are ready to receive you as emperor and to do homage to you and promise to help you with all your affairs.' This news made King Arthur, Cligés, Fenice, and the barons very joyful. The king sent back the men-at-arms that he had summoned, and as soon as Cligés was able he made ready all he needed for his trip; he then took leave of the king and his friends and set out to sea with a good wind and kept on his way until he arrived at the port of Constantinople.

On his arrival, the city was immediately filled with people who came before him in a fine procession and received him with great honor and led him to the palace. He wed Fenice and was crowned, as was she, with great glory, for there was no one who was not well pleased with Fenice. Upon Cligés's accession to the throne, many good things were done for the public good, but concerning the dances and other entertainment our account is silent. Yet we will see at the end of this story, in what follows, that Cligés was well loved by his people, as was Fenice. They established many chapels during their lifetime, and for their fine alms [p. 164] they were so loved by God that they had beautiful children. Once the children had come of age, Cligés and Fenice passed peacefully from this life, and their offspring – rather, the eldest son – had himself crowned. We shall make no mention of this but shall now conclude the present story transposed from rhyme to prose on the twenty-sixth day of March 1454.[36]

Expl*icit*

---

[36] The scribe has written 'IIII^c et LIIII' (454).

Glossary of Medieval Terms

ARMED: wearing armor (unarmed or disarmed: not wearing armor).

ARMOR: coif, hauberk, helmet, greaves, shield; lance, sword, spear.

ARMS: a term carrying several meanings, including (1) heraldic arms, (2) armor.

ARPENT: a unit of land measure equal to 0.85 acres.

BOHORT: an informal form of tournament or jousting, often impromptu and without being fully armed.

BOMBARD: the largest type of gunpowder artillery both in terms of weight (usually from five to ten tons) and bore; it fired stone balls.

BUISINE: a long straight horn with a flared bell; it is often depicted bearing a banner.

CANNON: possibly a generic name that in the early fourteenth century referred to all gunpowder weapons (except the bombard) before other names (e.g., veuglaire, coulovrine) came into prominence.

CANONICAL HOURS: times of the day (and night) laid out by the rule of Saint Benedict for prayers; the *Erec* and *Cligés* refer only to tierce and nones. Tierce (third hour after sunrise) falls around mid-morning, while nones (ninth hour after sunrise) is mid-afternoon. In the summertime in the north of France, tierce would be at about 9:00 a.m.; nones at about 3:00 p.m.

CHEMISE: a garment worn by both men and women under their outer clothing; the woman's was long, the man's shorter, coming about to the knees. Over the shift nobles wore a tunic; a woman then donned a robe or dress; a mantle often completed the outfit. In Chrétien's time clothing tended to be cut straight and loose; by the mid-fifteenth century it had evolved so that it was tighter-fitting.

COAT OF MAIL: a protective garment made of linked metal rings (mail) or of overlapping metal plates; hauberk.

COIF: a mail hood worn under the helmet.

COULOVRINE: a small hand-held piece of artillery that fired lead shot; of varying sizes, it was used with or without a stand or crutch.

CRAPAUDEAU (CRAPAUDINE): a long breech-loading, small-caliber gunpowder weapon.

COURSE (OF LANCE): in jousting, a run on the part of the two opponents against each other; a bout or round.

DENIER: a small silver coin of varying value—the twelfth part of a shilling (*sou*) or 1/240 of a pound (*livre*).

ENTREMETS: originally meaning a dish served between food courses, by the later Middle Ages it had come to refer to an elaborate dinner entertainment in the form of inedible ornaments or acted performances.

FALCON: see falconry.

FALCONRY (OR HAWKING): a sport practiced among the nobility in the Middle Ages, involving the keeping and training of birds of prey to permit themselves to be handled and hunt for small wild game. Different types of falcons or hawks were used; they are differentiated by their size, sex, and wingspread. The *Erec* and *Cligés* refer to four kinds of birds: the sparrow hawk, a smaller bird; the goshawk, a large, powerful bird; the tercel, a male; and the falcon, a female.

GOSHAWK: see falconry.

GREAVES: leg armor.

GREEK FIRE: an incendiary material used in medieval warfare, described as able to burn in water; first used by the Byzantine Greeks.

HARNESS: the complete outfit of armor.

HAUBERK: the basic piece of armor, it was a long-sleeved shirt of mail extending to the knees; in the fifteenth century plate armor gradually replaced mail.

HELMET: headgear that evolved over the course of the Middle Ages so that the knight's head was completely enclosed and protected during battle.

HIPPOCRAS: a sweet spiced wine.

MARK: an eight-ounce weight used to measure gold and silver.

MELEE: a mass tournament, fought between two sides, often on an open field.

NONES: see canonical hours.

PALFREY: a saddle horse, usually for women to ride.

POURPRE: a dark, luxurious material.

ROUND TABLE (TO HOLD): provide food for all comers.

SADDLE-BOWS: the arched upper front and back parts of the saddle; they were quite high and wide, so that the rider was firmly ensconced in the saddle.

SALLET: a rounded, metal helmet with a projecting guard for the neck and often a visor.

SENESCHAL: an official in medieval noble households responsible for overseeing domestic arrangements and servants.

SPARROW HAWK: see falconry.

TERCEL: see falconry.
TIERCE: see canonical hours.
TREBUCHET: a catapult for hurling heavy stones.

VEUGLAIRE: a piece of artillery considered medium-sized (up to 8 feet long and weighing up to several tons), it had a smaller chamber than the bombard and was larger than the crapaudeau.

Select Bibliography

Selected Editions

Chrétien de Troyes. *Cligés*, ed. Stewart Gregory and Claude Luttrell. Cambridge, 1993.

Chrétien de Troyes. *Erec et Enide*, ed. Jean-Marie Fritz. In Chrétien de Troyes, *Romans; suivis des chansons avec, en appendice, Philomena*. Paris, 1994.

Christian von Troyes. *Sämtliche erhaltene Werke*, ed. Wendelin Foerster. Halle: vol. I, *Cligés* (1884), prose *Cligés*, pp. 281–338; vol. III, *Erec et Enide* (1890), prose *Erec*, pp. 253–94.

Colombo Timelli, Maria, ed. *L'Histoire d'Erec en prose: roman du XVᵉ siècle*. Geneva, 2000.

——, ed. *Le Livre de Alixandre Empereur de Constentinoble et de Cligés son filz: roman en prose du XVᵉ siècle*. Geneva, 2004.

Pickford, Cedric E., ed. *Erec, roman arthurien en prose publié d'après le MS fr. 112 de la Bibliothèque Nationale*. 2nd edn, rev. Geneva, 1968.

Dictionaries

Dictionnaire du Moyen Français (1330–1500). DMF version 2009. http://www.atilf.fr/dmf.

Greimas, Algirdas Julien, and Teresa Mary Keane. *Dictionnaire du Moyen Français*. Larousse. Paris, 2001.

Hindley, Alan, Frederick W. Langley, and Brian J. Levy. *Old French–English Dictionary*. Cambridge, 2000.

Selected Translations

Chrétien de Troyes. *Arthurian Romances*, trans. William W. Kibler [*Cligés*, *Yvain*, *Lancelot*, and *Perceval*] and Carleton W. Carroll [*Erec and Enide*]. London, 1991; rpt with rev. bibliography, 2004.

The Complete Romances of Chrétien de Troyes, trans. David Staines. Bloomington, 1990.

Lacy, Norris J., gen. ed. *Lancelot-Grail: The Old French Arthurian Vulgate and Post-Vulgate in Translation*. 5 vols. New York, 1993–6; paperback rpt 10 vols. Cambridge, 2010.

Critical Studies

Abramowicz, Maciej. *Réécrire au Moyen Age. Mises en prose des romans en Bourgogne au XVe siècle*. Lublin, 1996.

Amor, Lidia. 'Chrétien de Troyes en el siglo XV: la prosificación de *Cligés* en la corte de Borgoña'. *Estudios sobre la traducción en la Edad Media*, ed. Leonardo Funes, María Silvia Delpy, and Carina Zubillaga. Buenos Aires, 2009. Pp. 79–110.

——. 'La presencia del mito tristaniano en *Cligès* y en el *Livre de Alixandre empereur de Constentinoble et de Cligés son filz*'. *Medievalia*, 39 (2007). Pp. 48–62.

Bakelaar, Bette Lou. 'Certain Characteristics of Syntax and Style in the 15th-Century *mises en proses* of Chrestien's *Erec* and *Cligès*'. *Semasia*, 3 (1976). Pp. 61–73.

——. 'From Verse to Prose: A Study of the 15th-Century Versions of Chrestien's *Erec* and *Cligès*'. Diss. Ohio State University, 1973.

Barber, Richard, and Juliet Barker. *Tournaments. Jousts, Chivalry and Pageants in the Middle Ages*. Woodbridge, 1989.

Barrois, Joseph. *Bibliothèque protypographique ou Librairies des fils du roi Jean, Charles V, Jean de Berri, Philippe le Bon et les siens*. Paris, 1830.

Bogdanow, Fanni. 'The Fragments of *Guiron le Courtois* Preserved in MS. Douce 383, Oxford'. *Medium Ævum*, 33 (1964). Pp. 89–101.

Bohler, Danielle, *et al*. *Le Goût du lecteur à la fin du Moyen Âge*, ed. Danielle Bohler. Paris, 2006.

Cartellieri, Otto. *The Court of Burgundy*. New York, 1929.

Cazauran, Nicole. 'Les romans de chevalerie in France: entre "exemple" et "récréation"'. In *Le Roman de chevalerie au temps de la Renaissance*, ed. Marie-Thérèse Jones-Davies. Paris, 1987. Pp. 29–48.

Chartier, Roger and Henri-Jean Martin. *Histoire de l'édition française*. Vol. I: 'Le livre conquérant. Du Moyen Age au milieu du XVIIe siècle'. Paris, 2nd edn 1989.

Chase, Carol J. 'The Devil is in the Details: Enide's Clothes in the Burgundian Prose *Erec*'. Paper presented at the 44th International Congress on Medieval Studies. The Medieval Institute of Western Michigan University, Kalamazoo, MI, May 2009. Article forthcoming.

Chaytor, H. J. *From Script to Print; An Introduction to Medieval Vernacular Literature*. Cambridge, 1950.

Colombo Timelli. Maria. 'Cherchez la ville: Constantinople dans la littérature narrative "bourguignonne"'. In *Sauvez Byzance de la barbarie du monde*, ed. L. Nissim and S. Riva. Milan, 2004. Pp. 113–30.

——. 'Le *Cligés* en prose (1455), ou l'actualisation d'un ancien *conte* en vers'. *L'Analisi linguistica e letteraria*, 8 (2000). Pp. 327–40.

——. 'Le *Conte d'Erec*, roman bourguignon du XVe siècle - Quelques problèmes d'édition'. In *Le Moyen Français. Le traitement du texte, édition, apparat critique, glossaire, traitement électronique*, ed. Claude Buridant. Strasbourg, 2000. Pp. 65–80.

——. 'De l'*Erec* de Chrétien de Troyes à la prose du XVe siècle: le traitement des proverbes'. *Le Moyen français*, 42 (1998). Pp. 87–113.

——. 'Entre *histoire* et *compte*: de l'*Erec* de Chrétien de Troyes à la prose du XVe siècle'. *Les Lettres romanes* (1997), special issue. Pp. 23–30.

——. 'L'*Erec* en prose – ou quelques traces de l'implication du lecteur dans un roman du XVe siècle'. In *Le goût du lecteur à la fin du Moyen Age*, ed. Danielle Bohler. Paris, 2006. Pp. 117–32.

——. '*Erec* et *Cligés* en prose: quelques repères pour une comparaison'. *Le Moyen Français*, 51/52/53 (2002–2003). Pp. 159–75.

——. 'Expressions de temps et progression de l'histoire dans "l'Histoire d'Erec", roman en prose du XVe siècle'. In *Temps et Histoire dans le roman arthurien*, études recueillies par Jean-Claude Faucon. Toulouse, 1999. Pp. 75–82.

——. 'Fictions de vérité dans les réfections en prose d'*Erec* et de *Cligés* (XVe siècle)'. Colloque 'Fictions de vérité dans les réécritures européennes de Chrétien de Troyes' (Rome, Academia Belgica, April 2010). Forthcoming.

——. 'L'Histoire d'*Erec* en prose du manuscrit Paris, B.N. fr. 363 (ff.193r°b–222r°b) – Quelques remarques'. *'Por le soie amisté': Essays in Honor of Norris J. Lacy*, ed. Keith Busby and Catherine M. Jones. Amsterdam, 2000. Pp. 149–61.

——. 'Mémoire linguistique dans les réécritures arthuriennes des XVe et XVIe siècles'. Colloque 'Temps et mémoire dans la littérature arthurienne' (Bucharest, May 2010). Forthcoming.

——. 'Les mots de la courtoisie dans quelques romans et adaptations en prose du XVe siècle'. Plenary lecture. 'Cultures courtoises en mouvement' – XIIIe Congrès de la Société Internationale de Littérature Courtoise (July 2010). Forthcoming in the Congress proceedings.

——. 'Pour une "défense et illustration" des titres de chapitre: analyse d'un corpus de romans mis en prose au XVe siècle', in *Du roman courtois au roman baroque*, ed. Emmanuel Bury and Francine Mora. Paris, 2004. Pp. 209–32.

——. 'Sur l'édition des mises en prose de romans (XVe siècle): bilan et perspectives'. *Le Moyen français*, 44/45 (1999). Pp. 87–106.

——. 'Syntaxe et technique narrative: titres et attaques de chapitre dans l'*Erec* bourguignon'. *Fifteenth-Century Studies*, 24 (1998). Pp. 208–30.

——. '*Talanz li prant que il s'an aille*: le v. 5056 du *Cligés* de Chrétien de Troyes et l'invention d'un prosateur du XVe siècle'. In *Favola, mito e altri saggi. Studi di letteratura e filologia in onore di Gianni Mombello*. Alessandria, 2004. Pp. 359–75.

——, et al., eds. *Mettre en prose aux XIVe–XVIe siècles*. Turnhout, 2010.

Deschepper, Catherine. 'De l'adultère comme résistance à l'empereur usurpateur... La convergence des intrigues amoureuses et politiques dans le *Cligès* en prose'. In *La Littérature de la cour de Bourgogne, Actualités et perspectives de recherche*. Ed. Claude Thiry and Tania Van Hemelryck. *Le Moyen Français*, 57/58 (2005–2006). Pp. 67–86.

——. '"Mise en prose" et "translation". La traduction intralinguale des romans de Chrétien de Troyes en moyen français'. Thèse de doctorat. Louvain-la Neuve, 2003.

De Winter, Patrick. *La Bibliothèque de Philippe le hardi, duc de Bourgogne (1364–1404)*. Paris, 1985.

Di Stefano, Giuseppe. *Dictionnaire des locutions en moyen français*. Montreal, 1991.

Dixon, Rebecca. 'The Wedding Reception: Rewriting the Ideological Challenge in the Prose *Cligès* (1454)'. *Cahiers de recherches médiévales*, 14 (2007). Pp. 315–26.

Doggett, Laine E. *Love Cures. Healing and Love Magic in Old French Romance*. Penn State Romance Studies. University Park, PA, 2009.

Doutrepont, Georges. *La Littérature française à la cour des ducs de Bourgogne; Philippe le Hardi, Jean sans Peur, Philippe le Bon, Charles le Téméraire*. 1909; rpt Geneva, 1970.

——. *Les Mises en prose des épopées et des romans chevaleresques du XIVe au XVIe siècle*. 1939; rpt Geneva, 1970.

Godzich, Wlad and Jeffrey Kittay. *The Emergence of Prose: An Essay in Prosaics*. Minneapolis, 1987.

Grimbert, Joan Tasker. 'The Fifteenth-Century Prose *Cligés*: Better Than Just Cutting to the Chase'. *Arthuriana*, 18.3 (2008). Pp. 62–72.

——. 'Love and War in the 15th-Century Burgundian Prose *Cligés*: The Duke of Saxony's Passion for Fenice'. In *War and Peace: New Perspectives in European History and Literature, 700–1800*, ed. Nadia Margolis and Albrecht Classen. Berlin. Forthcoming.

Gunn, Steven J., and Antheun Janse, eds. *The Court as a Stage: England and the Low Countries in the Later Middle Ages*. Woodbridge, 2006.

Haidu, Peter. *Æsthetic Distance in Chrétien de Troyes: Irony and Comedy in 'Cligès' and 'Perceval'*. Geneva, 1968.

Jones, Catherine M. *Philippe de Vigneulles and the Art of Prose Translation*. Cambridge, 2008.

Kaeuper, Richard. 'The Societal Role of Chivalry in Romance: Northwestern France'. In *The Cambridge Companion to Medieval Romance*, ed. Roberta Krueger. Cambridge, 2000. Pp. 67–114.

Keller, Hans-Erich. 'The *mises en prose* and the Court of Burgundy'. *Fifteenth-Century Studies*, 10 (1984). Pp. 91–105.

Kjaer, Jonna. 'Cligés et Fenice, un couple d'amoureux exemplaires dans le *Cligés* en prose du XVe siècle, roman bourguignon'. Forthcoming in *Le Moyen Age*.

——. 'Les complaintes d'Enide dans l'*Histoire d'Erec en prose*, roman bourguignon'. In *'Contez me tout': Mélanges de langue et de littérature médiévales offerts à Herman Braet*, ed. Catherine Bel, Pascale Dumont and Franck Willaert. Leuven, 2006. Pp. 243–58.

Krueger, Roberta L. 'The Author's Voice: Narrators, Audiences, and the

Problem of Interpretation'. In *The Legacy of Chrétien de Troyes*, ed. Norris J. Lacy, *et al.* 2 vols. Amsterdam, 1987. I, pp. 115–40.

——, ed. *The Cambridge Companion to Medieval Romance*. Cambridge, 2000.

Lachet, Claude, ed. *L'Œuvre de Chrétien de Troyes dans la littérature française: réminiscences, resurgences et récritures*. Lyon, 1997.

Lacy, Norris J. 'Adaptation as Reception: the Burgundian *Cligés*'. *Fifteenth-Century Studies*, 24 (1998). Pp. 198–207.

——. 'Arthurian Burgundy: The Politics of Arthur'. In 'Late Medieval Arthurian Literature', in *The Arthur of the French. The Arthurian Legend in Medieval French and Occitan Literature*, ed. Glyn S. Burgess and Karen Pratt. Cardiff, 2006. Pp. 494–6.

——. 'Motivation and Method in the Burgundian *Erec*'. In *Conjonctures: Medieval Studies in Honor of Douglas Kelly*, ed. Keith Busby and Norris J. Lacy. Amsterdam, 1994. Pp. 271–80.

——, and Joan Tasker Grimbert, eds. *A Companion to Chrétien de Troyes*. Cambridge, 2005.

——, *et al.*, eds. *The New Arthurian Encyclopedia*. New York, 1991; rev. 1996.

Laurioux, Bruno. 'Banquets, entremets et cuisine à la cour de Burgogne'. In *Splendeurs de la Cour de Bourgogne: récits et chroniques*, ed. Danielle Régnier-Bohler. Paris, 1995. Pp. 1027–127.

Loomis, Roger Sherman, and Laura Alandis Hibbard Loomis. *Arthurian Legends in Medieval Art*. New York, 1938.

Marchello-Nizia, Christiane. 'La forme-vers et la forme-prose: leurs langues spécifiques, leurs contraintes propres'. *Perspecives médiévales*, 3 (1977). Pp. 35–42.

——. *Histoire de la langue française aux XIVe et XVe siècles*. Paris, 1979.

——. 'Ponctuation et "unités de lecture" dans les manuscrits médiévaux'. *Langue française*, 40 (1978). Pp. 32–44.

Ménard, Philippe. 'La Réception des romans de chevalerie à la fin du Moyen Âge et au XVIe siècle'. *Bulletin Bibliographique de la Société internationale arthurienne*, 49 (1997). Pp. 234–73.

Middleton, Roger. 'Index of Former Owners'. In *Les Manuscrits de Chrétien de Troyes / The Manuscripts of Chrétien de Troyes*, ed. Keith Busby, *et al.* 2 vols. Amsterdam, 1993. II, pp. 87–176.

Paris, Gaston. '*Cligès*', ed. Foerster. *Romania*, 13 (1884). Pp. 441–6.

——. '*Erec et Énide*', ed. Foerster. *Romania*, 20 (1891). Pp. 148–66.

Pearson, David. *Provenance Research in Book History: a Handbook*. London, 1994.

Piponnier, Françoise, and Perrine Mane. *Se vêtir au Moyen Age*. Paris, 1995. Eng. trans. Caroline Beamish, *Dress in the Middle Ages*. New Haven, CT, 1997.

Porter, Pamela. *Medieval Warfare in Manuscripts*. London, 2000.

Quéruel, Danielle. 'Des mises en prose aux romans de chevalerie dans les collections bourguignonnes'. *Actes du VIe Colloque International sur le Moyen Français*. 3 vols. Milan, 1991. II, pp. 173–93.

——. 'La naissance des titres: rubriques, enluminures et chapitres dans les mises en prose du XVe siècle'. In *À plus d'un titre. Les titres des œuvres dans la littérature française du Moyen Age au XXe siècle*. Lyon, 2001. Pp. 49–60.

Rasmussen, Jens. *La Prose narrative française du XVe siècle. Étude esthétique et stylistique*. Munksgaard, 1958.

Roques, Gilles. 'Les variations lexicales dans les mises en prose'. In *Mettre en prose aux XIVe–XVIe siècle*, ed. Maria Colombo Timelli, *et al*. Turnhout, 2010. Pp. 9–31.

Schnerb, Bertrand. *L'État bourguignon 1363–1477*. Paris, 1999.

Smith, Robert Douglas, and Kelly DeVries. *The Artillery of the Dukes of Burgundy 1363–1477*. Woodbridge, 2005.

Szkilnik, Michelle. 'Le prince et le félon: Le siège de Guinesores dans le *Cligès* de Chrétien et dans la prose bourguignonne'. *Cahiers de recherches médiévales*, 24 (2007). Pp. 61–74.

——. 'Medieval Translations and Adaptations of Chrétien's Works'. In Lacy and Grimbert, eds, *A Companion to Chrétien de Troyes*. Pp. 202–13.

Taylor, Jane H. M. 'The Significance of the Insignificant: Reading Reception in the Burgundian prose Cligès'. In *Fifteenth-Century Studies*, 24 (1998). Pp.183–97.

Thiry, Claude, ed. *'À l'heure encore de mon escrire': aspects de la littérature de Bourgogne sous Philippe le Bon et Charles le Téméraire. Les Lettres romanes*, special issue (1997).

——. 'Les mises en proses: bilan des études philologiques'. In *Mettre en prose au XIVe–XVIe siècles*. Turnhout, 2010, ed. Maria Colombo Timelli, *et al*. Pp. 53–64.

Thiry-Stassin, Martine. 'Interventions d'auteur dans le *Cligés* en prose de 1454'. In *Hommage au professeur Maurice Delbouille*. Special issue of *Marche romane* (1973). Pp. 269–77.

Vale, Malcolm. *War and Chivalry: Warfare and Aristocratic Culture in England, France, and Burgundy at the End of the Middle Ages*. London, 1981.

Vaughan, Richard. *Philip the Good: The Apogee of Burgundy*. London, 1970; new edn: Woodbridge, 2002.

——. *Valois Burgundy*. London, 1975.

Wallen, Martha. 'The Art of Adaptation in the Fifteenth-Century *Erec et Enide* and *Cligès*'. Diss. University of Wisconsin, 1972.

——. 'Significant Variations in the Burgundian Prose Versions of *Erec et Enide*'. *Medium Ævum*, 51 (1982). Pp. 187–96.

Willard, Charity Cannon. 'Chrétien de Troyes, Burgundian Adaptations of'. In *The New Arthurian Encyclopedia*, ed. Norris J. Lacy, *et al*. New York, 1996. Pp. 91–2.

——. 'The Misfortunes of *Cligès* at the Court of Burgundy'. In *Arturus Rex*, ed. W. Van Hoecke, G. Tournoy, W. Verbeke. 2 vols. Leuven, 1991. II, pp. 397–403.

Index

ARTHURIAN STUDIES